Dancing uphill

Dancing uphill

The cycling adventures of Charles Holland,
the first English rider in the Tour de France

Frances Holland

publishing

For Alastair, Melissa, Philip, Fiona, Claire,
Faye, Amy and Sarah, with love

First published in 2007 by
M&N publishing
4 Brunswick Road
London W5 1BD

Reprinted in 2008

www.m-and-npublishing.co.uk

A catalogue record for this book is available from the British Library

ISBN 978-0-9555676-0-5

Created by M&N publishing
Editor: Nina Holland
Designer: Martin Hendry

Printed in Spain by Grafo Industrias Grificas

Every effort has been made to ensure that the information
contained in this book is factually correct, however, there
may be some inaccuracies, for which we apologise.

Contents

Foreword

I have always been infatuated with cycling. My father, Joe, was a keen cyclist and a member of the Central Roads Club where he won time trials. He took me to see lots of cycle races, particularly as Wolverhampton, where we lived, was the hub of cycling – many of the races started and finished or passed through there, such as the Brighton to Glasgow and the Tour of Britain. At the age of eleven, Dad and I cycled to the Halesowen track to watch, among others, British sprint World Champion, Reg Harris, in action.

When I was fourteen I joined Wolverhampton Wheelers and began riding in club time trials. I also enjoyed competing in the weekly track league meetings at Wolverhampton's Aldersley Stadium. At this time, I would scour any cycling magazines I could get hold of to learn about the races I was later to take part in, including the Tour de France, the most gruelling event in the sporting calendar.

In those early years, like the rest of the cycling fraternity, I followed with interest the careers of such greats as Fausto Coppi, Brian Robinson, Tom Simpson, Louison Bobet and Jacques Anquetil, who were all my heroes. I didn't know too much about British pre-war riders, but I'd heard that Charles Holland, a fellow Midlander, had ridden in the Tour de France.

I didn't know Charles personally, although my father may have come across him in the 1930s when he was racing. It seems, however, that we share several cycling experiences. We both took up cycling because of our fathers' interest in the sport and both enjoyed different aspects of the sport – on the road and on the track. Coincidentally, we both broke our collarbones during a London Six-day event, and many of the places we visited and cycling events we competed in, such as the Olympic Games and the Tour de France, were the same – except, of course, my achievements were over thirty years later.

Cycling still preoccupies me and I'm fortunate enough to be able to report and commentate on the current generation of cyclists. However, I think it's fitting, that Frances and Nina have compiled this book, which includes Charles' memoirs, his

Hugh Porter racing to his second world title in 1970 at Saffron Lane, Leicester.

dispatches from the Tour, and other articles he wrote. It will help to ensure that British cycling traditions and a past generation of cyclists are not forgotten.

HUGH PORTER MBE
Four times World Pursuit Champion

Introduction

What do you do with a large suitcase full of cycling memorabilia? Neatly kept records of race times, distances and winners (dating from 1928), magazines, press cuttings, photographs, programmes, invitations, menus and contracts were only a part of the contents. Olympic and Tour de France shirts and caps, medals galore and two handwritten exercise books of memoirs, all told a story.

We knew that our father had taken part in the Olympic Games and the Tour de France but not a great deal about his cycling career. The cabinet full of silverware at home had always been there and was just a part of the furniture. When trying to sort out

the contents of the suitcase, after his death, it became clear there was a story behind all this and one we thought worth telling.

Charles' father, Walter, was a keen cyclist as were his brothers, Walter (junior), Alfred and Jack. While cycling may be a father-to-son sport, it is not a father-to-daughter sport – at least not in our case. We are not 'cyclists' (although we do ride bikes) and

are aware that cycling books are generally written by sports journalists or cyclists (amateurs, professionals and 'bikies'), but as Charles had written so much himself and had many articles published we decided to put it all together for posterity.

In the 1930s cycling was predominantly a male pursuit, although some women did take it up. *Cycling* magazine discussed its pros and cons in 'Girls and Cycling Clubs'. It took the form of an interview: 'If you were a mother would you let your daughters join a cycling club and chase all about the countryside with a lot of boys?' The advice given was: 'Let the protected young womanhood ... enjoy the healthiest and the most enjoyable method of interesting leisure ... the moral standard of club cyclists is remarkably high.' Obviously, Charles didn't read this!

They may have high moral standards but, 'with all due respect', cyclists and particularly club cyclists seem to be a breed alone, often fanatical about bikes and the 'bike game'. Charles was no exception, and his memories of the early years (chapters 1 and 2, written in the 1960s) include numerous accounts of races – dates, times and statistics. He believed that every race counted and he kept notes of what happened, detailing what went right and what went wrong. He analysed his own performance as well as his opponents in order to keep ahead of the game.

In addition to recording his performances, his memoirs give a glimpse of the whole pre-war cycling scene, which was based around the clubs, the camaraderie between cyclists and the unique 'education' that cycling gave to him.

At the time the cycling calendar was fairly constant and between March and September, many races had specific dates, such as the Anfield '100' held in May, often on Whit Monday, or the Manchester Wheelers '12-hour' held in September. Cyclists would also meet up regularly to race on grass or cinder tracks in cricket

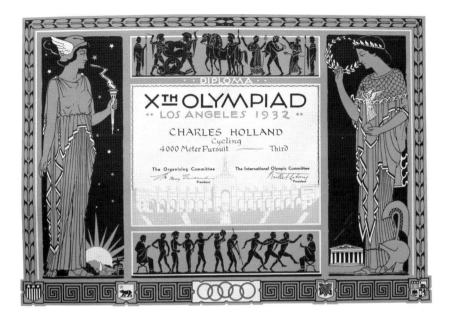

grounds or in sports clubs. Track racing on grass took place at 'sports days', which were often organised by factories, collieries, or even the local gas works. Charles entered many of these, such as the one held locally at Bournville, Birmingham.

The cycling year always ended with the annual dinner and prize presentation, which Charles fondly refers to in his memoirs. After he died we attended one such dinner held by the MC&AC to celebrate their centenary. One of the rituals at this most formal of events is the cross-toasting, which takes place after the speeches and formal toasts. We experienced this quaint custom for ourselves and were happy to 'take wine with' various club members who had known the Holland brothers.

Most athletes aspire to represent their country and, once Charles had been noticed by 'headquarters' (cyclists also have their own language, see page 9), he did so at the Olympic Games, firstly in

Los Angeles, 1932, and secondly at Hitler's infamous Games in Berlin, 1936. These events were in total contrast to one another, but just like the Games in recent years, they were surrounded by controversial aspects (such as the selection processes) and political issues. In 1932, never before had a team of cyclists undertaken such a long journey for their country, and in 1936 no-one had an inkling that these would be the last games for twelve years.

Charles enjoyed all aspects of the 'bike game' and, during the period between the Games, he established himself as a best all-rounder in terms of all types of cycling – time trials, mass starts and track racing. It took him to the World Championships in Leipzig; a trip to Denmark; and a race around the Tuileries.

After ten years as an amateur – and a great deal of blood, sweat and tears – in 1937, Charles turned professional and accepted an invitation to take part in the world's toughest bike race, the Tour de France. He had no idea of what was in store, the very thought of riding in the Tour was awe-inspiring. Within a few days he was the loneliest man of the Tour, without team support or direction. He experienced the snow and freezing cold of the mountains, the heat and sweltering sunshine of the Riviera, the drudgery of cycling in the wind and the rain, the exhaustion of climbing the mountains and the hazard of the downhill run. Imagine riding 2,991 kilometres over fourteen days, often in unfavourable conditions with no manager, trainer, technical advisors,

In 1938 Charles took part in the professional road race at the World's Championship in Amsterdam and Valkenburg.

or even friends to talk to – 'with no help at all, you might say'.

However, it was a thrilling experience and great adventure and, after a day of incredible physical endurance, Charles had the energy to write an account of his gallant attempt. Written in the style and language of the day, he comments on how wonderful the scenery is and how pleasant it is seeing 'bathing beauties' in the South of France. He certainly

Charlie enjoyed socialising, having a cigarette and a beer.

enjoyed himself, while taking part in this most gruelling of races.

After the Tour, Charles continued as a professional, riding for Raleigh/Sturmey-Archer – 1938 was the year of professional records, including the Liverpool to Edinburgh and Lands End to London. Unfortunately, World War II cut short his career. It was not until the 1960s that he took up cycle racing again. Nothing made him happier than returning to amateur status as a veteran. This enabled him to ride to victory once more. He was referred to as a 'super-vet' who set records in 25-, 50- and 100-mile events 'with the pedals flowing as freely as ever'.

Throughout his career Charles always provided the press with good copy, whether it be in respect of his cycling ability or even his looks (very 'non-pc'). In his early career he was described as having 'raven hair as sleek as molten tar and a melting brown eye that brings every bird off the twig for miles around Walsall …' When he narrowly missed a record it was, 'Charlie, the sacrifice on the altar of red tape'. Naturally, we think he was well worth the copy, hence his distinguished cycling career is documented here.

NINA HOLLAND

In the mid-1930s, the Holland brothers were a well-known team of racing cyclists, from left to right: Walter, Alf, Charles and Jack.

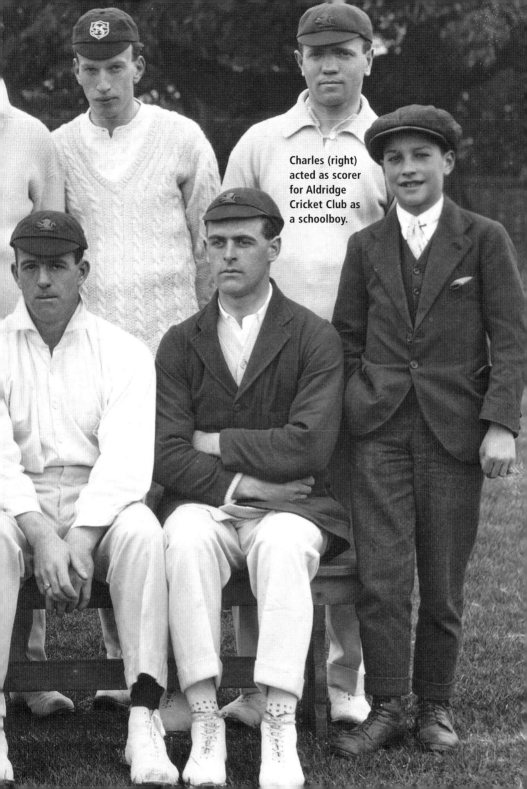

Charles (right) acted as scorer for Aldridge Cricket Club as a schoolboy.

CHAPTER 1
Memoirs of a cyclist

Charles was born in the village of Aldridge in Staffordshire in 1908, at that time, a place where everyone knew practically everyone else who lived there. In the early 20th century Aldridge prospered, mainly due to farming, brick making and coal mining. Coal was first found in 1874. Charles' father, Walter, came to Aldridge from Yorkshire in around 1900 to put electricity in the coal mines. The pits were closed in 1936 as they proved to be uneconomical. Nevertheless, Aldridge grew considerably in the 1920s and 1930s and even more so after the Second World War, but, as Charles himself noted, right up until the 1960s it maintained a rural atmosphere. It boasted a railway station (closed in the 1960s), a thriving high street with two pubs, and several schools in the area. For many, community life centred around St Mary's Church (founded in the late-12th century), where Charles sang in the choir. In addition, there was a strong sporting tradition and the village had cricket, football and hockey teams. Against this background, Charles began his illustrious career.

" Cycling has meant and still means a lot to me and I think I have indulged in most branches of the sport and thoroughly

The Aldridge Old Boys football team in the 1925–26 season. Charles is seated in the second row on the far right.

enjoyed all of it, not that cycling was my first love. Football and cricket were undoubtedly the most popular of all sports during the early days and to play these games for a living was a boyhood dream. I first played for the Aldridge Schoolboys after the end of the First World War, and joined the Aldridge Cricket Club juniors section about the same time. I acted as scorer for a couple of years, but often played, if someone failed to turn up.

Jack Mathews who wrote a book entitled, *Aldridge Cricket*, had as great a part as anyone in any sporting attributes I may have acquired. He was a master at the Aldridge Schoool and ran the football and cricket teams. His connection with the cricket club extended over 50 years. He always went out to win, but he had to win fairly, and would stamp down on any boys trying to get away with anything dubious.

I was playing in the cricket team regularly at seventeen years and was very proud to be playing with such distinguished players as Howard Walton the Captain, who played for Staffordshire, and Dr V. E. Milne the Aston Villa footballer, who also played cricket for Scotland. I packed up football, when the 'Villa' failed to show any interest and started to play hockey and had got to the stage of being asked to have a trial for the county.

Both my father and eldest brother, Walter, were interested in cycling and this interest rubbed off on me. The Walsall Polytechnic Cycling Club (later Walsall Roads) was less than four miles away and my father became a member in those early days. He didn't

Aldridge hockey team around 1930. Charles (pictured second row right) started playing hockey after giving up football. His brother, Walter, is seated front row second from the right.

do a lot of racing but for a time held the Walsall–Matlock record. He loved pottering around the beautiful countryside and when Walter was nine years old, he bought him a juvenile bicycle and proceeded to show him the joys of cycling. After two or three years Walter had a new adult bike and the 24-inch wheel bike was handed down to me and subsequently to my younger brothers, Alfred and Jack.

How many thousands of miles this little bike did I don't know but several pairs of new tubes were fitted. Dad always kept an eye on it, to see that it was oiled regularly, the bearings properly adjusted and the roller type brakes always efficient. That we all sat a bike well should be taken for granted. Long before Jack had grown too big for the junior model, Walter had joined the CTC (Cyclists Touring Club) and rode regularly with the Walsall section.

New horizons were now regularly appearing before us. We were very familiar with places such as Tamworth, Lichfield, Cannock and the hundreds of villages and hamlets to the north and east of our village, and we were thinking about cycling further afield. Walter regaled us with stories of places such as Loughborough where the wonderful magical bells tolled in the New Year and drew cyclists in hordes to ride through the night to listen to them, and of the rocky dales beyond Ashbourne, where the River Dove majestically flows through breathtaking scenery.

At school we had a pretty good grounding in geography and history, and in my early cycling days it seemed that the object of the lessons were mainly for cyclists. Similarly, it was as though the Romans had built the carefully routed Watling Street (now the A5) for us cyclists. Thousands used it on their way to spend a weekend or week's holiday in North Wales and, except for an occasional herd of cows or a muck cart, the cars were few and far between, and it was commonplace to see groups of 25 or so on club runs.

Hoteliers and inn keepers had for a long time appreciated the benefits to be had from the cycling fraternity and prominently displayed plaques supplied by the CTC and NCU (National Cyclists Union) to show their approval of the amenities offered. It's a pity that these inns of hospitality have disappeared, and the convivial conversation to be had there has succumbed to the blare of the juke box and television.

I didn't do much touring as much of my time was taken up with local activities. Looking back, I often wonder how we managed to fit everything in. We lived a mile from the local school, so even at five years old we walked four miles backwards and forwards, and as we got older, we would go back for cricket or football practice. Then there was choir practice or the boys club. On Sundays, particularly in the summer, we went to Sunday School in the morning and the evening, with long walks through the fields, in between or after the services, so ten or twelve miles would be commonplace.

My great, great grandfather was one of the best walkers. My mother told me the story of how he used to walk to Walsall and back to fetch the mail; this was before the railways were built through Aldridge. By the time he'd delivered it, I reckon he'd done up to twenty miles. The family ran the Post Office in those days.

I think I must have been about twelve years old when I went on my first cycling tour. Dad, Walter and myself went up to Chester. We stayed at a CTC guesthouse that was full of riders mainly from the Liverpool area. All travellers are good talkers and cyclists are no exception but we did manage to take a walk around part of the old city walls and the quaint tiered shops. Dad had to return home the next day but Walter and I cycled to the Wirral, and visited an Aunt at West Kirby, then over to Birkenhead to have a look at the docks, and back to Chester for another night at the guest house.

Setting off the next morning, I got involved with a pony and trap. I don't know exactly what happened, but I thought the pony shied and backed into me and the board, which went over the wheels, caught me just under the left eye and made a nasty cut. I had it dressed at a nearby chemists and rode home with this huge bandage around my head peering through with my right eye.

It had bled pretty well and I must have looked in a terrible state. On arriving home, the local nurse who lived nearby started to clean it up ready for dressing. Why I don't know but I just passed out. The verdict was that I had a weak heart so even at that early age I had to play everything just a little bit harder to prove her wrong.

Around three years later in 1923, my next cycle tour began. My pal Les and I set off and got as far as Evesham the first day. We had a night there and then made our way down the Wye Valley ending up near Hereford. We got fixed up at a little pub, had a meal and sampled the local cider. To this day I've never been able to find that pub with the leaning walls and sloping floors again. It was all most enjoyable.

Walter by now had designs on a tandem, the first one was a second-hand 'ladyback' [designed for a lady to ride on the back], with a single gear of around 68. I was invited to join him on CTC runs and we enjoyed these tandem rides, but Walter got rid of it when he was persuaded to have a go in a 25-mile event.

Bernard Satchwill was on the scratch mark of this '25' run by the Warwick Road club – a club formed by CTC members in the Midlands during the early 1920s. Walter pedalled his way around the course on a 76 gear to win fairly easily with a course record of 1 hr. 9 min. 37 sec. This was the first bicycle race I had seen, and right away I felt I must have a go. I had a fairly old sports-type machine but I'm afraid it was not suitable for racing and, of

Charles and his brother Walter, left (wearing matching black tights and alpaca jackets) after breaking the Midland RRA 50-mile tandem record with a time of 1 hr. 53 min. 54 sec. in 1929.

course, in those days I was not considered old enough and Dad was very firm about this.

By 1925 my mileage was growing considerably and on one occasion I rode through the night to Pangbourne to see the Etna 50-mile time trial. My front tyre had a hole in it, but a piece cut out of an old outer cover placed under the hole made it rideable, but only just, as it bumped all the 200 miles there and back. I think it was the bumping that kept me awake that long night. Frank Southall, who had really set the game alight, won the race.

By this time I was cycling backwards and forwards to south Birmingham where I was working, and was feeling pretty fit. I took on all and sundry up Barr Beacon hill, the highest point in south Staffordshire, and rarely lost a battle, mind you it was only by racing home that my working day was inside twelve hours. As soon as I changed and fed, it was cricket practice or the concert party. Yes, Walter and I used to perform duets, such as *The Gendarme Duet* or the *Two Beggars*. Walter had a good baritone voice and I got by as the tenor. Winter or summer there was always something to do, debating, dances, arranging or practising for concerts. I was glad when Saturday night came and I could have a quiet drink after the match with the hockey or cricket boys, although that would often finish up with a singsong.

Walter training for a 50-mile race organised by the MC&AC. He was considered to be among the best twelve riders in the country at this distance.

Looking at my brother's 1927 fixtures list, I saw Wyndham Novices 25-mile time trial was due to take place. Borrowing Walter's bike, I have a go and finish second in 1 hr. 10 min., a local lad named Majos beat me by a few seconds. I didn't hear of him again, I wonder why? The winners of these events usually go on to big things. However, one or two of my pals at Aldridge started to fancy their chances, so I got entry forms for the next local open event which was the Walsall Imperial CC 25-mile time trial.

The secretary wanted to know the name of the club we were riding for. I said on the spur of the moment 'Aldridge Imps'. He asked, 'Who's the secretary?', 'I am', I replied, 'and who's the treasurer', he asked. 'I am',

I said, and so a week or so later Les Wickstead, Arthur Roberts and myself faced the starter in the colours of Aldridge's first cycling club. We didn't do too badly in this Sunday morning event. I think I suffered the most as I had played cricket on the Saturday afternoon and I soon found, that chasing after balls was not very clever before a cycle race.

The Walsall Roads '30' time trial was our next effort, and this followed the same pattern as before, a cricket match on the Saturday, and more suffering, but I'd just got the edge on the others. We had one more ride that year, having a go in the Burton '25'. Freddie Brown of the Pottersure Cycling Club won with a time of 1 hr. 7 min., which was considered pretty good then. I was third with 1 hr. 9 min.

I was invited to join the Midland Cycling and Athletic Club (MC&AC) and have never regretted accepting. The membership was full of characters, with quite a few who had started cycling on the old penny farthing. One such character was Frank Urry. Like his father, John, Frank was a brilliant writer and poet, a very shrewd legislator and a diplomat with a kindly nature. In addition to running two businesses, he was a CTC councillor, contributing regularly to the cycling papers. It would be difficult for me to say where Frank Urry did his finest work for cycling, but his work on a government transport commission was never fully appreciated by cyclists.

My first cycling success came on 1 April 1928 when I managed to beat the scratchman Syd Woods in the Walsall Roads Club 10-mile time trial. My next event was a '15' time trial also run by the Walsall Roads. The Roads had great expectations of Harry Archers a real flyer at the shorter distances. I was one of the earlier starters and after finishing stood just back from the finish, waiting to see whether Harry could beat my 39-minute ride. He put in a terrific

A studio photograph of Charles, the aspiring cyclist, with his first racing bike.

finish, and in the heat of the moment ducked his head, and swerved across the road, I managed to throw myself aside at the last moment as he was about to hit me, and the only damage was my smashed front wheel.

I was delighted with my winning ride and was looking forward to a good 25-mile ride against J. K. Middleton, B. Satchwell, F. Greenwood and my brother Walter, all riders considered to be among the best twelve in the country at 50 miles. I won the handicap prize in this event and was only half a minute behind J. K. M. on actual time, both of us doing 1 hr. 4 min. This was a Tuesday evening event and so for once I was not worn out by the running about at the Saturday cricket game.

I started to take an interest in track riding by this time, spurred on by the track lads one would frequently meet training on the road. A few clubs seemed to specialise in track riding, and although there wasn't a fast track in the Midlands, bar the peculiar-shaped cement track at Derby, trackmen were well catered for by the many cycling and running sports days held on cricket grounds and cinder tracks. Besides the terrific bursts of speed acquired by trackmen in the short distance races, usually between a quarter of a mile and five miles, riding ability was considerably higher on the track. One also required plenty of nerve, when in a bunch, to offset the many different tactics employed by the opposition. I found it a fascinating game once I had got over the novice stages but I certainly felt a bit of an idiot in those early days.

My first attempt at track racing was at the sports day organised by the Metropolitan Carriage Works of Birmingham. This was held on their sports ground at Washwood Heath. The first event was a handicap on the quarter-mile circuit around the cricket ground. I'm afraid I hadn't really got moving before most of the back markers had passed me. I went better in the next half-mile event and passed a few in the straight, only to have them all sweep by on the inside as I ran wide on the bend.

I must have gradually improved my technique because I won several events towards the end of that season. I was the only rider in the MC&AC doing track-riding, and they tried to discourage me from straying as it was considered detrimental to the time trialling on the road. However, I enjoyed both events, although having only one bike I seemed to spend a lot of time, taking off or putting on brakes and mudguards, changing tyres on the sprint wheels for the different surfaces (Dunlop made special tyres for the grass tracks), and then after the weekend sport, the bike would be converted back for its utility use.

There were several other time trials I managed to enter during the season, including the Walsall Roads '30' in which I did the fastest time, and the Midland '50' when I came third fastest. This led to my selection to ride for the MC&AC in the annual 50-mile match against the London Polytechnic on the Worcestershire course. It was in this event that my brother Walter rose to the occasion to win, and so made the huge Bennett Cup his own property, having won the race twice before. I was very pleased with my third place, as being in the winning team, I received my first gold medal.

My last race in 1928 was a 50-mile time trial again run by the MC&AC. Jack Middleton of the London North Road Club was on scratch. He was one of the best twelve 50-milers of the year and had not so long returned from Amsterdam, where he had ridden in the Olympic Games road race. You may imagine my delight when starting two minutes after him I caught and passed him in the last few miles of this '50'. It was a great incentive to me and there and then, I made up my mind, God willing, to be part of the Great Britain team for the next Olympics in Los Angeles. With four years in between the games, I had plenty of time to prepare, but I decided I must finish completely with cricket and hockey, and concentrate 100 per cent on cycling.

It seemed the most wonderful thing that had ever happened to me when I received notice that I had been selected for the Games to ride in both track and road events. However, a lot of water passed under the bridges before that came about. After my first real season of racing I found most of the experienced riders relaxed a little during the winter months and so I supported the social side of club life and the weekend runs. These and the riding between home and business meant that a reasonable measure of fitness was maintained.

The breaks on a run, for elevenses, lunch or tea, were often of a very entertaining nature with effervescent youth bubbling over with the joys of living and naturally the older members could always rely on a quiet corner for their discourses on the amusing anecdotes on club life over the past 30 odd years. Current affairs, naturally, in those difficult years had a share in the proceedings, and everyone enjoyed themselves in the analysis of the day's controversies, political or otherwise.

Most clubs usually had an Annual Dinner and Prize Presentation, but the Midland club, having a large membership and a number of other sporting activities to contend with, namely motorcycling, cricket and golf, had a separate function for the cycling presentations coupled with a concert. It was at the annual cycling 'do' in January 1929 that the Celtic Serenaders, a choir of Welsh miners singing for the benefit of their poverty-ridden, workless valley, asked permission to entertain us. Words fail me to describe the atmosphere in that room as the Welshmen went through their repertoire. It was magnificent. They certainly deserved the contributions collected, which no doubt matched the fees of the professional artists engaged.

Charles' younger brother, Alfred, congratulates him at one of the many track meetings they both attended.

CHAPTER 2
Learning the bike game

❝ The start of the 1929 season found me far from being as fit as I should have been, I felt good and strong, but my first few events were not by any means up to the standard I had set myself. I won a couple of 25-mile time trials in moderate times, but my rides in the '50s' were very poor.

I was doing a fair amount on the tracks and I suppose I had not as yet acquired the versatility necessary to switch from the sprint to the longer time trials. I spent the Whitsun holiday in May doing the tracks, riding in the 500-yard and half-mile handicaps at the gas works' sports day in Birmingham. I won nothing, but gained a little more valuable experience. I also entered the sports day at Ellesmere in Shropshire, but as the trains were not suitably timed I decided to ride there. I had to cycle about 55 miles at almost 20 mph from Wolverhampton to get there on time. However, loaded with racing kit and mudguards fitted, I just didn't quite make it, and it was only with the help of some of the lads who prepared my bike, while I changed, and the starter being prevailed upon to wait a few seconds that I made the heats of the second race. How I got to the final I just don't know but I won a 3rd prize as a consolation. Albert White, possibly the world's greatest grass-track rider in his prime, won the major prizes that day.

Albert was riding at the Rover Meeting at Coventry the next day and, when I mentiond I had also entered, I was offered a lift home. Mick McCormack had the car; a man whose life was cycling, a rider in the days of Viv Johnson, the 1908 Olympic Champion. Mick was not in Vic's class but the work he did for the NCU (National Cyclists Union) as a judge and legislator was almost full time. He became president of the NCU in 1930.

The track at Coventry was moderately banked, with a new and faster surface, which seemed to suit me. It was my first time there, and in the three-quarter-mile handicap I won my heat and cross-heat well, and really felt confident when I won the final from a good field. I was also riding in the 3-mile 'point-to-point' and, after one or two skirmishes, broke away from the bunch and almost lapped the field.

The following weekend I entered the Walsall Roads '30' but I still couldn't get moving the way I wanted to and had to concede success to my brother, Walter, who was riding well considering that he was doing a fair amount of studying at the time. It was towards the end of June when I next showed a glimpse of form by winning the MC&AC '50' by more than two minutes over a difficult hilly course with a time of 2 hr. 18 min., equalling the course record.

I was certainly learning the hard way, and when I accepted an invitation to ride in the National 25-mile Championship on the Derby track, after being boxed in, I soon found myself well behind the leading bunch. The other riders in the same predicament called it a day and I was chasing alone. The crowd gave me a little half-hearted applause, no doubt thinking I should soon be lapped, but I suppose the leaders eased a bit, and so I tried that bit more and the gap got a little less. The crowd really got to work then, and they just roared me along, my lungs seemed ready to burst and my legs about to fold, when I finally caught the leaders. I'm afraid I had no sprint left for the finish but I was able to collect my lap prizes that I had won in the early stages.

On the following Tuesday evening I won the MC&AC '25' in the then fastest-ever time of 1 hr. 4 min. 2 sec. on roads in the Midlands. By now I felt that I had acquired the peak of fitness (although performances in later years seem to put a doubt on this) and I didn't need much training in between events, as they were held fairly frequently. The next event, for instance, was on the following Saturday. It was the annual 50-mile match between the MC&AC and the London Polytechnic and took place on the North Road starting at Biggleswade, the London club being the hosts on this occasion. We went by train to Bedford and then cycled across to the start. We soon realised that we were in for a tough ride, as the half gale sweeping the flat countryside was treating the tall grain most unkindly.

The alleged experts didn't think anyone would beat 2 hr. 20 min. on the day, but I went through in 2 hr. 17 min. my fastest up till then. Walter did 2 hr. 19 min. for second place and third place went to a rider from the Polytechnic doing 2 hr. 25 min. Once again the MC&AC won the team medals. These events were always good fun, and after a bath and a good meal we were all set for a jolly evening. This occasion followed the usual pattern and needless to say we needed no rocking to sleep. The next morning there didn't appear to be any need for hurrying, and after a real cyclist's breakfast, the 90 miles home was as pleasant a ride as one could wish for, a little different to some of the 'bashes' in which racing cyclists get involved.

I rode at quite a few more track meetings that year, mostly on grass and with varying degrees of success in the handicap races, which are most popular at these meetings.

The MC&AC was organising a 100-mile event in the middle of August and I thought I would have a ride just to get the feel of the great distance. I had planned to 'tour' the first 50 miles and I certainly kept to the plan finishing in 5 hr. 10 min. It was considered then quite a reasonable ride, but I certainly didn't hurt

myself, and when the next '50' came along a week or so later I did my best ride to date, winning with a time of 2 hr. 14 min. which was a course record.

Walter had now bought another tandem, one built by Joe Cooke and, although second-hand, it was in fine condition. The Birchfield Cycling Club had organised a 50-mile tandem event, and Walter and I decided to ride in it. We had one or two training rides and went to the start feeling fairly confident on our 90-fixed gear. The course took place on the Watling Street, starting and finishing by the Parson and Clerk pub near Sutton Park. The 25-mile point was about five miles short of Wellington. We had quite a good ride and won fairly comfortably in a few seconds over 2 hours.

The Birchfield event gave us the confidence to attack the Midlands Road Record Association (MRRA) Unpaced Tandem '50', which we did although it was almost at the end of the season. We managed to beat the existing record by 10 minutes in spite of a puncture, necessitating the changing of a tyre; the time was 1 hr. 53 min.

The course that was most usually used for these record attempts started on the outskirts of Bristol and went north through Gloucester and then turned north east at Tewkesbury. My outstanding memory of this ride was the scare I got on the descent of the hill in Thornbury with the sharpish bend, almost at the bottom, how we negotiated

Charles takes the lead in the annual sports day event at Bournville (home of Cadburys), near Birmingham, racing on a grass track.

the bend, at the terrific speed we were doing, I just don't know. I was on the back seat, my legs were flying around, but I was keeping the back steady, Walter did the rest. The art of tandem riding is 'nicking' together – I think we demonstrated our ability in that respect in more ways than one.

Another pleasing side of my riding in 1929 was the team pursuit competition. As the MC&AC didn't compete in the National Team Championships, I rode with the Walsall Roads Club. We had a fine team comprising Syd Woods (captain), George Gray, Lew Bensley and myself. We won the Midland Championship and made the final at the Meeting of Champions at Herne Hill. Although beaten by the Norwood Paragon team (the Southall brothers and Hellebeck) the Walsall Club were so very pleased Jack Aspinall, the President, presented us with gold club badges.

I suppose it is fair to say that I had had a reasonably good season in 1929 but with my ambition to be selected for the Los Angeles Olympics in mind, I decided I must not relax too much.

The Walsall section of the CTC had inaugurated a cross-country race between cyclists and harriers. It was first held in 1923 and the honours had been fairly evenly divided amongst some of the best runners and riders in the Midlands. I was delighted with the invitation to compete in the 1929 event, and more so when the November weather, though cold was dry, and so was advantageous to the cyclists. Quite big crowds gathered at the finish, and at various vantage points on the course, and by using the faster roads cyclists could see the race at half way, and beat the competition back to the finish. My track riding ability coupled with my time trialling stood me in good stead and I came in first. The crowd beyond the finishing line had closed in, funnel like and the cinematography news cameraman was right in the middle and being a fast finish I just couldn't help hitting him.

I found out later at the cinema just how they managed to show objects seemingly coming off the screen and into the auditorium.

The MC&AC club runs were well supported about this time, and up to 30 members would sometimes sit down to tea. One run to the Cotswolds through Bideford, Weston-Subedge and Moreton-in-the-Marsh, across the valley to the Edge Hills and then down to Long Compton, would be a least 70 miles, which constituted good training especially on the homeward run, even though it would be done in the dark. I found night riding very pleasant on occasions. The hum of tyres on the better-surfaced roads was sweet music in our ears in the quiet of the night. No one could appreciate the seasons more than the cyclist, whose regular riding contributed to a fitness to enjoy the summer and winter, the spring or autumn, or just day and night.

Of course, being a racing cyclist called for a lot more than cycling just for the fun of it and, once the New Year was with us, I needed to watch my diet to see that there was no over abundance of the wrong eats and drinks. Breathing exercises and other physical training are called for and, most important of all, plenty of rest. I always tried to get nine hours of sleep, when you train hard I think it's necessary for recuperation.

I certainly started the 1930 season fitter than on previous occasions. My club decided to send a team to the Highbury 50-mile time trial at Easter, held on the North Road, so popular with the North London club. Jack Lanterwanes, the then current British 50-mile record holder, was the favourite but it wasn't his day and, in spite of the wintry conditions, I was the fastest individual with a time of 2 hr. 17 min. 24 sec., and with Jack and Syd Middleton we won the team event. This was my first win in an open event promoted by a London club and I suppose it was natural that 'headquarters' now started to take a little more notice of me.

I continued mixing my racing between the road and track, and was now becoming a more complete rider, and received plenty of invitations for scratch races on the track and other specialised events. One such race at Bournville sports day (a crowd of 10,000 enthusiasts attended this event) was a pursuit match against Frank Southall and his brother Monty. Billy Bricknell rode on my side and we won fairly easily. Monty was not so good on a grass track as on a cement one. Everyone has to take a number of beatings in whatever sport you take to and I think there's a lot to learn here. I had one in the Warwickshire Roads '50' when Joe Bragg came up with a flyer, and I was relegated to second place.

It was on the Shropshire course where I did my best '50' in 1930. The Manchester Wheelers were the promoters, a club that were supreme in running cycle events, whether on the track or road, sprints, 10 miles, 50 miles or 12 hours. They must have brought more world champions together in competition than most other clubs put together. There were no world champions to my knowledge, competing in this 50-mile event, but most of the best 50-milers from the Midlands and North were there.

It was with some trepidation that I faced the time keeper at the start of this twice round, 25-mile triangular-shaped course and, as usual, didn't really start moving until the first circuit had been completed. However, on this pleasant afternoon as the warm June sunshine got brighter, one couldn't help but give of their best, at least that is how I found it, and I went on to do the fastest time in 2 hr. 13 min. 28 sec. This time it was Reg Middleton who joined Syd and myself in claiming the team medals.

After the event I was invited to join the Wheelers for a 'run' to Wem, where they had booked a hotel for the weekend. What an evening that was, as mixed a crowd as one could get, half

Frank Southall and Charles were both team-mates and rivals in the 1930s.

professional and half tradesmen but all truly great cyclists. They fêted me in grand style during the meal, and I was one of them in the revelry that followed, never out of hand but never a dull moment. When I asked to be excused, not wanting to be too late for bed, the doctor of the party insisted that I had a room to myself so that I'd lose no sleep after my day's exertions. Considering the numbers that were there for the night, it was a kind thought that I greatly appreciated.

The 50-mile match with the London Polytechnic was the following weekend, and it was held on our rather hilly course. It suited me and I had a fairly easy win, but the Londoners just couldn't get moving on it, their fastest being 6 minutes behind.

My success in the 50-mile events brought me an invitation to compete in the North Road CC Memorial '50' for the best twelve riders in the country. I was looking forward to another ride on the North Road, but came unstuck. G. W. Jerkins of the Hastings Cycling and Athletic Club was the winner with a ride of 2 hr. 11 min. I was 2½ minutes slower, but as I had crashed at the track sports at Aylesbury on the previous Thursday I wasn't as fit as I should have liked to have been.

The MC&AC like most of the old clubs always thought of road racing in terms of '100s' and 12 hours. The '25s' were considered training rides and '50s' were appreciated to show one's speed and a build up for the '100s'. Given my recent successes in the '50s', it was not surprising when I found myself kidded into having a go in the Speedwell Bank Holiday '100'. I had not thought of riding this distance until the following year, but relented under the pressure.

Bren Orrell of the Anfield CC was on scratch, he was one of the three chosen for the World Championship that year, and right from the word go he established a lead. I was 3 to 4 minutes slower at 50 miles, at 82½ miles the difference was 1 minute 20 seconds, and at 96 miles it was down to 40 seconds. I got another 18 seconds off in the last 4 miles, but the 22 seconds left made Bren a good winner, with a course record of 4 hr. 47 min. I had the consolation of winning the handicap prize, because no one including myself thought I had a chance for the fastest prize, as this was my first serious ride at the distance.

The season of 1930 was fast coming to an end, in fact I had no races of importance to worry about. I felt that I had achieved a step nearer my ambition and entered one or two of the remaining fixtures in a very carefree manner. I won one Midland '25' and was second in another.

About this time Albert Lusty reminded me of a win that Frank Greenwood and I had had earlier in the season in the Wood End Tandem '50'. Teaming up with Frank was due to the fact that my brother Walter was not in training and neither was Albert, Frank's former partner. Frank was racing before I was born, and although he was not in his prime he still had a nice turn of speed. We had a few training rides, and when it came to the race we really showed them how, not quite as fast as Walter and I, but fast enough to beat the rest. Albert had suggested that Frank and I went for a Midland Road Record. So we teamed up on the tandem once again, with the MRRA '100' as our objective. It was not the most demanding ride, but it was acclaimed as a great performance when we beat the record by 10 minutes.

One thing I am certain of was that in spite of the difficult times in those days, we really had fun. The wonderful camaraderie of the cycling fraternity was really something. When Frank and I returned from our tandem rides, mother always fixed us a good meal, and the banter that went on during that hour had the house in an uproar. It was Walter's tandem we were using and comments such as 'the tandem seems to be going faster than ever' from Mother would really set things going, maybe only tandemists would realise the subtlety of it.

The winter of 1930–31 seemed to pass exceedingly fast. The weekends were usually taken up with club runs and we did quite a fair mileage. At the start of the New Year, I made a practice of getting back earlier, maybe before lunch or tea depending on where we had gone. The idea was to get a fast ride home. I cannot remember the exact details of my training schedule at the time. I suppose I was getting so many theories on the subject, that I became a little frustrated. I started the new racing season reasonably fit but with no real edge on the speed, and what with a batch of punctures I didn't achieve much for quite a while. I continued to mix my racing on the road and on the track; it was really a means to an end, that of becoming a complete bike rider.

I didn't get an invitation to ride in the 1931 North Road '50', as my best form came too late for that, but won at least five '50s' and two '100s' in an unbeaten run towards the end of the season. I won the Rover '50' in 2 hr. 14 min., but my best '50' was in the Coventry Godiva event, which I won by 6 minutes, on a day when most riders were 2 minutes slower than in the Rover event, yet I was 2 minutes faster with a time of 2 hr. 12 min.

My greatest win that year was undoubtedly the North Road '100'. I was very confident after my recent run of successes including the Midland '100', and was not worried when I found myself a minute or two down at 50 miles, knowing we had a very tough finish. In spite of this I finished in the event record time of 4 hr. 43 min.

I suppose my form during the past season was partly upset by my unsatisfactory employment. Like many others during the late 1920s and early 1930s I had been made redundant, after working for practically nothing during my apprenticeship of seven years. I then tried several other jobs but finally settled down as a representative in the cycle trade for Hercules. I enjoyed it and met a lot of cycle agents up and down the country and by now I was in a position to understand and help in the intermingling of the utility, the tourist and the racing trade. I was determined to be in top form for the early races of the coming Olympic year and so kept a rein on my social activities, exercised, and did a fair mileage regularly.

Interestingly, it was in 1932 that our present Queen had her first bicycle. It was a birthday present from the Cycle Manufacturing Union to, as she was then, Princess Elizabeth. According to the magazine *Sport and Play*, between 40 and 50 manufacturers took part in a draw, similar to the Irish Sweepstakes draw, with a revolving drum and numbered balls, for the honour of building the machine or supplying parts of it. By request no announcement was made of the draw, to the general press, and the destination of the bicycle was not disclosed to the workers engaged in building it.

Olympic fever was prevalent from the opening of the 1932 season. Trials were being held at the various tracks, and the time for the 1,000 metres and other distances were being very carefully studied. I observed Bill Harvell, Stan Chambers (the Brighton policeman) and Frank Southall had all put up good times at Herne Hill. I had done the fastest 100 metres on the slow Alexander Ground Track in Birmingham and, of course, the Wyld brothers of Derby, who had ridden the 4,000-metre team pursuit in the 1928 Games, were still a force to be reckoned with. The road race at Los Angeles was to be a time trial, and I was informed that a win in the forthcoming Anfield '100' would be a useful aid to selection.

The Warwickshire Road '50' was my first event, in what was to me a memorable year. The times were slow due to the shocking weather, but my 2 hr. 16 min. 23 sec. was good enough to beat Percy Stallard, Joe Brays, Len Cave and a host of others, who were in with a chance. A 10-mile event run by the Rovers gave me a chance to show a bit of speed and another win. This was followed the next weekend by a win in the MC&AC '50'

In 1932, three weeks after winning his first Anfield '100', Charles won the BSA Gold Vase, against stiff opposition.

and with a few extra training miles I was feeling quite happy about the Anfield Whit Monday '100'.

The club run to Shrewsbury on the Sunday prior to the race was a pleasant diversion and we settled into our quarters at The Wardol. After the excellent evening meal we had a stroll around this very interesting old town, called at The Castle to greet the Anfielders and, after more greetings with the many cyclists who seemed to have taken over the town, I was pleasantly tired and ready for bed, conscious of the morrow's ordeal.

The ride of 6 miles to the start at Shawbury even at this early hour soon made me realise that this classic event had drawn spectators and supporters from miles around. It had rained heavily throughout the night but had stopped for the race itself. The roads were still very wet and on one of the corners I slipped on the loose surface of the road. I came down but managed to remount without too much delay and I was happy to win this classic event in 4 hr. 48 min. for the first time.

I had been invited, and accepted, to ride in the 10-mile scratch race that was to be held three weeks later at Bournville. The trophy for this was the BSA Gold Vase, worth about 100 guineas, and one of the most valuable athletic trophies at this time. With three wins, a rider could make this handsome prize his own and A. White (Rover CC), S. Chambers (Brighton CC) and C. Gauden (Crescent Wheelers) each already had two 'shares'. At the start with them were 15 other top riders and the crowds of about 6,000 waited in eager anticipation for the off.

T. W. Blick (Birchfield) and I started setting a good pace, taking lap prizes pretty much alternatively. With three miles to go we managed to lap the field. In the last 300 yards Blick pulled away but I was on his wheel and a final spurt put me in first position. The spectators were delighted that a local person had won.

Charles proudly
wearing a Union
Jack on his shirt
for the first time.

CHAPTER 3
La vie en rose

Throughout the early 1930s Charles had his sights set on being selected for the Olympic Games in Los Angeles and he must have been extremely upset and concerned when he read an article in *Cycling* magazine, 3 June, entitled, 'Someone has blundered'. It began, 'What are the real chances of English cyclists participating in the Olympic Games? Is it fair to the riders in training and the general public that uncertainty should reign until this late hour?' However his fears were unfounded, exactly one month before the team were due to set sail the names of five cyclists were announced. Much to Charles' delight, he was selected, along with Frank William Southall, William Harvell, Stanley Meredith Butler and Ernest Alfred Johnson. The MC&AC wasted no time in contacting him and, along with their congratulations, asked him to write his story for their magazine *The Roll Call*.

The cost of the trip and the problem of raising funds had made the selection of the British team even more difficult than usual, particularly as the Council of the British Olympic Association had decided the previous July, 'that no competitor who is unlikely to reach the semi-final or final of his event shall be taken to Los Angeles and that only the absolutely necessary officials shall be taken'. It was finally agreed that a total of 72 competitors and officials would travel at an estimated cost of £150 per head.

For the cyclists, this meant that instead of a full team of twelve to cover the different events, seven were finally selected. Out of the five that were initially chosen, Southall, Harvell, Butler and Holland were entered in the 100-kilometre road race, and Southall, Harvell, Johnson and Holland in the 4,000-metre team pursuit. Harvell would also ride in the one-kilometre time trial. The other two members of the team were the Chambers brothers. Ernest H. Chambers was to ride in the sprint event and again in the tandem race with his brother, Stanley (Jerry) Chambers.

It was reported in *Cycling* on 13 July 1932, 'Amid scenes of wild enthusiasm the team of seven cyclists left Waterloo for the first stage of their epic journey. The crowds, the mountains of luggage, the three big crates containing the machines, the hissing steam and the shrieking whistles, the bubbling joviality, all blended into

Smartly dressed in their Olympic blazers and slacks, the Los Angeles cycling team and two officials, eagerly await the start of the Games.

one big picture that will be for ever memorable.' It appears that Holland and Harvell, grinning like naughty school boys, were seen disappearing up the platform to see the Hungarian girl athletes who were travelling with them.

At Southampton docks Lord Burghley, the captain of the British team, met the ex-Prime Minister Stanley Baldwin, who was leading a large group of delegates to the Imperial Economic Conference in Ottawa. The politicians and the athletes met with 'a mutual desire to do their best for home and Empire' and boarded the *Empress of Britain* with high expectations of what lay ahead.

On their way to the Olympic Games, the cyclists trained on rollers on board the *Empress of Britain*.

The trip to Quebec was a wonderful experience for Charles. On board were the British contingent (apart from the boxers and the swimmers who sailed a week later), the South African, Belgian and, of course, the Hungarian teams. The Canadian team were to join the group in Toronto.

In order to keep themselves fit, the cyclists used training rollers on the deck and played the various deck sports that were on offer. Unfortunately, someone managed to dent the rollers and so they were only able to ride on a six-inch strip, which made a somewhat difficult training regime even more tricky.

Charles wrote to *The Roll Call* magazine, as requested, and this is his account of the voyage.

" Dear Mr Urry

This is our third day at this hotel in Toronto, the biggest in the British Empire, it is some place.

Our trip across the Atlantic was wonderful, our meals on board particularly good, although a lot of the boys were unable to do justice to them through sickness. I personally felt fitter than ever. The log book describes the sea as being rough, although it seemed calm to what I have read about.

There were several exciting incidents aboard. A fire broke out in the Empress Room but, fortunately, there was not much damage, most of it was caused by water. Later in the fog, we nearly sank a collier from Middlesborough, it hit our bows slightly damaging the plates. The collier rocked very badly but righted itself as the crew rushed for the boats badly scared.

The *Empress* attempted a record crossing but, owing to fog, we were forced to drop anchor, and arrived in Quebec several hours late. As we crossed the points opposite Abraham Heights we were greeted with aeroplanes, other boats all over the harbour, and sirens hooting; the din was deafening.

Our trip from Quebec to Toronto was done in sleeping cars during the night.

Our first training spin proved disastrous. Stan Butler of Norwood Paragon, skidded in the tram lines, and went under a car; the wheels did not pass over him, but he was dragged along; he had two or perhaps three ribs broken, cuts and bruises. Some think he may be able to ride; I don't think so.

We have something to do all the time. For instance, yesterday after I went for a little spin in the morning, we went around a cycle factory, then to a girls' baseball match, followed by another reception where Lord Burghley presented prizes to Canadian Olympic girls, and from there to an all-in wrestling match. We have other country teams with us, namely Belgians, Hungarians, South Africans and New Zealanders, it is very interesting watching various games being practised.

I have now got to start packing for Chicago, so cheerio and remember me to all the boys, who I hope are winning all the team races.

All the best Charlie H.

The hotel Charles referred to in Toronto was the Royal York. It was surprisingly sumptuous for a group of British cyclists and, as Frank Southall wrote, 'every man a room to himself, every room two beds, a bathroom attached, telephone and wireless etc.'. The only downside was that 'the boys got lonely and chummed up in pairs'.

As regards the trip to the cycle factory in Toronto, in an interview given to a Birmingham newspaper on his return from the Olympics Charles recalled his visit. 'As a factory it was splendid but the bicycles produced were, with one exception, heavy and ungainly. Most of them were modelled on motorcycle designs with twin-front forks, and double-top tubes and reinforced handlebars. The exception was the really well-designed light-weight machine built up from fittings made in Birmingham.'

The next stage of the itinerary, from Toronto to Los Angeles, was a five-day train journey with a stop off in Chicago. According to the *Chicago Daily News*, Friday 22 July, 200 athletes were met that day from the train and then taken to the Lakeside Athletic Club for a workout and a swim. This was followed by a tour of the city and the World Fair grounds, and a dinner. Rushing about in yellow cabs and having an armed police escort, with blaring sirens, was a thrilling first for the cyclists.

Following the fun in Chicago, the teams took the Santa Fé train to Los Angeles. It departed at 11.45 a.m. and although the

carriages were 'ice cooled' it was extremely hot. The windows were kept closed and opening one for a breath of fresh air was just like opening a furnace. Shorts and singlets were the fashion for this part of the journey. After a few days on the train, a stop of four hours was made at Alburquerque. The runners wanted to train but the cyclists were not allowed to due to the 'lightness' of the air. Instead they spent their time, boating, swimming and enjoying themselves besides a lake. Finally, they arrived in Los Angeles where they were greeted by well-wishers before boarding coaches which took them to the Olympic village.

For the first time in the history of the Olympics the male competitors were housed in a single village while the women stayed in a luxury hotel. At the village, set in over 300 acres, each nation had its own area. Competitors were housed in two-bedroomed rose-coloured cottages, which were surrounded by lawns and flower beds. Also on the site was a hospital, post office, library and a large number of different eating places. In Charles' own words:

" The Olympic village is situated in the Baldwin Hills and overlooks Los Angeles. Miles away at the back of the town are mountains and it is a fine view. The roads around are usually crowded with sightseers and autograph hunters but they are not allowed inside. It is guarded by police and cowboys ride the boundaries.

Since we left England we have seen no rain, and if it were not for the houses the place would be like a desert. Fruit is the only thing that is cheap here. There are so many things to talk about, such as the wonderful opening ceremony and some of the brilliant feats that have been achieved, but I must leave these for a later date. "

Every Olympics is different and each has difficulties to overcome. Taking place during the depression years of the 1930s, and with the cost of travel to the comparatively remote city of Los Angeles so high, six months before the Games were due to start, there had been no replies to the official entrance invitations. Once they had started to trickle in, the next problem was the sale of tickets to fill the enlarged Memorial Coliseum stadium, which held 105,000 people. This picked up only when stars such as Douglas Fairbanks, Charlie Chaplin, Marlene Dietrich and Mary Pickford offered to entertain the crowds. Still, the world of the Olympic Games was changing and, although there were only half as many competitors as in the 1928 Olympics, the Los Angeles Games saw the start of the razzmatazz we know today.

The opening ceremony attracted 100,000 spectators, although

by today's standards it was very low key. There was no lighting of the flame ceremony and mascots were unheard of, but several ground-breaking techniques were introduced. Automatic timing for track events was used for the first time, as was a photo-finish camera. The result of a final was changed after judges had seen a

film of the race – this had never happened before. Medal winners had a podium to stand on and the flag of the winner was raised. The close proximity of the main stadium to Hollywood meant that many movie stars of the day attended. Furthermore, in the interest of international goodwill, although the Games took place during Prohibition, an exception was made for the French and Italian teams who were allowed to import and drink wine – they argued that it was an integral part of their training diet. In total 37 countries were represented; 1,408 athletes, of whom only 127 were women, would compete in fourteen different sports.

The Los Angeles Games were the first to last sixteen days, from 30 July to 14 August and since then all summer Olympics have lasted between fifteen and eighteen days. The track cycling events held at the Rose Bowl, Pasadena were scheduled for 1–4 August. Training, sight-seeing and enjoying American hospitality occupied Charles and the rest of the team until the racing began.

About 9,000 spectators attended the first evening at the Rose Bowl, and this figure doubled by the second and third days. Charles' first event, the 4,000-metre team pursuit, was held on the evening of 2 August. The broad track was well-designed and constructed and all the cycling events that took place on it were closely contested. This race was no exception and it was reported as 'a thriller'. The teams started on opposite sides of the track, the object being to catch the opponents or to complete the ride in the fastest time, with the official time being that of the third rider.

In the first heat the British team had been drawn against the Americans who they beat with about three laps to go. They then had a decisive win over the Canadians. Finally, they were up against the French team, who had beaten all records in training and were expected to win this event. Riding well and with three laps to go they had a slight lead when Johnson, who was in second

Charles and the rest of the team
(Frank Southall, William Harvell,
Ernest Johnson) photographed
at the Rose Bowl, Los Angeles,
after winning bronze in the
4,000-metre team pursuit.

place, punctured. This unfortunate stroke of bad luck made all the difference and they were beaten by a fraction of a second. The gold medal was won by the Italians (who set an Olympic record of 4 min. 52.9 sec. in the heats) in 4 min. 53 sec. The silver went to the French in 4 min. 55.7 sec. and the bronze was awarded to the British team with a time of 4 min. 56 sec.

Interestingly, the tradition of winning an Olympic bronze medal in the team pursuit continued up until 1956 in Melbourne where it was won for the sixth consecutive time. The legendary Tommy Simpson was in this team.

Heralded as the fastest thing in the Olympic Games, the 100-kilometre (62.14 mile) road race took place on Thursday 4 August at 8.00 a.m. As the official programme states:

Standard racing type cycles are used. There are two railroad crossings on the course at which timers will be stationed to record the actual time a rider may be delayed by passing trains, the total time out at railroad crossings for this reason to be deducted from such contestant's elapsed time.

More than a score of motorcycle officers will patrol the course and the public is urged to keep off the course as much as possible. Contestants will be disqualified if a motor car travels in front of them as a pacer. Such a practice would serve as a wind break and give contestants added advantage.

Three official cars will patrol the course, carrying one representative of each of the competing nations.

Each rider will carry with him on the handlebars of his cycle a two-place container for liquid refreshment. Riders carry a spare tyre lashed to their shoulders. Rules forbid riders to take food from sources other than those carried with them unless they dismount. Since the race is against time, contestants may pause whenever and

Stanley Butler, Frank Southall, Charles Holland and William Harvell prior to the 100-kilometre road race.

as often as they desire. No rider may follow another closer than 25 metres or come closer than 2 metres from another in passing.

The road race started some 50 miles from the Olympic village near Moorpark passing through Somis, El Rio and Oxnard, before following the coast road, via Malibu, to the finish a few miles north of Santa Monica. Prior to the race, the British team had unfounded concerns that the Americans had little experience in organising this type of event – a time trial with the riders leaving at two minute intervals. In fact, the race was well organised and fairly judged. The course was kept absolutely clear by the police on high-powered motor bikes tearing after any cars that appeared and moving them out of the way.

The result of the race was disappointing for the British team. Southall did best coming in sixth, next was Holland who was fifteenth, followed closely by Stan Butler, who had made a determined recovery from his accident in Toronto and came sixteenth, and then Harvell who was nineteenth. The last of the starters, Attilio Pavesi of Italy, was the first home in 2 hr. 28 min. 05.6 sec. In all there were 35 starters of whom 32 finished.

In the post-mortem that followed a few things became clear. The

Some of the British althletes who took part in the Olympic Games arriving home at Southampton docks aboard the Empress of Britain on 26 August 1932. Charles is wearing plus-fours, popular with cyclists at this time.

British team, in comparison to the Italians, who had arrived six weeks before the race, had had very little time to acclimatise and the day of the race was very hot. More of a problem to Charles was the fact that since leaving England he had not had a massage and that as a result soon after the race had started his legs stiffened up. Charles wrote, 'I think we would all have done much better if we had been properly attended to.' With reference to this in an article entitled 'England's Losers', *Cycling* (9 September) reported, 'We impute no blame but one cannot help thinking of the costs of the expedition and how our chances of victory can be quite easily destroyed by some trifling factor.'

The remaining time in Los Angeles was spent relaxing, with visits to film studios and beach barbeques. The journey home via Salt Lake City, apart from a delay in Quebec of fifteen hours, was uneventful. Of the seven man team, Butler was unlucky as he was the only one returning without a medal. The Chambers brothers won a silver in their tandem race and the others had a bronze from the team pursuit.

Charles was not particularly proud of this, for him a medal meant gold.

At the end of the games the rose-coloured cottages of the Olympic village were dismantled. Caroline Walker, writing in the Los Angeles press, described it as the City of Dreams becoming a Dream City – something beautiful that is vanishing into the unreal. The cottages were to become holiday cabins in the mountains and along the coast, and the site allowed to return to its natural state. As she continued, 'Soon there will be only bare brown hills, thirsty for the slanting hues of the winter rains. But grey with mist or bright with sunlight there will never disappear from those hills the warm memory of friendships between the people of many nations permanently welded in those temporary cottages.'

A well-earned drink for Charles, who really appreciated the army of helpers at cycle races.

CHAPTER 4
Time trials and tribulations

Charles' last record attempt of the 1932 season was from Llandudno to Birmingham on 18 September. The wind was favourable, he began the climb of Ivesty Bank on Watling Street at 22 mph and his speed never dropped below 18 mph. He finished in Birmingham, remarkably fit, having completed the 117-mile journey in 5 hr. 29 min. 46 sec., beating the previous record by over 20 minutes. Unfortunately, this record time was rejected by the Midland Road Record Association (MRRA). This was due to the fact that Tommy Dilkes and Arthur Walker, also MC&AC members, were attempting a tandem record over the same route on the same day. They had set off from Llandudno 18 minutes before Charles, however, just outside Mold, their front tubular tyre became detached and the sprint wheel broke and they fell. Not badly injured and the tandem repaired they were able to continue. Unfortunately, this meant that Charles caught up with the tandem and 'the unpaced nature of the ride was open to grave doubt'. It was also reported by the MRRA that 'the following car was several times near enough for the timekeeper (acting as official observer) to give Charlie instructions, which the rules definitely state must not be done'. The MC&AC thought, 'it an unkind thing that Charlie should be the sacrifice on the altar of red tape'.

Charles finished the season in October by winning the 46-year-old North Road '100' for the second time. There were 96 entries for the race of whom 78 started and 50 finished. From the start, the task facing Charles was a difficult one, as among the starters were many well-known names. However, he knew the course and rode consistently, keeping wisely behind the leaders until the final 30 miles when riding into the wind he gave it his all. Charles riding on a free wheel did a winning time of 4 hr. 45 min. 15 sec. A. W. Brumell was second and P. T. Stallard third. Frank Southall, the Best All-Rounder of the year, retired after 60 miles with tyre trouble. The winning time was two minutes slower than Charles' first win in 1931, but the difference was almost infinitesimal compared with the variations in the weather. Ridden in a wind of nearly gale force that hindered much and gave little help, it was classed as one of the best rides of the year. It certainly justified his selection for the Olympic Games earlier in the year.

While cycling was taking up more and more of Charles' time, a quote from *The Roll Call* in January 1933 illustrates his continued interest in other sports: 'It is not only in road racing that Charles uses his head, he also uses it playing hockey. This we know for he attended a recent club run with a spread-eagled nose which somewhat spoilt the contours of his dusky beauty.' Presumably he had been hit with a hockey stick. Charles also found time to give interviews and when asked about how he would set about training a team for an international race, supposing he had autocratic powers, this is what he said:

> First of all I should choose a team in ample time before the date of the race so that the men could have every opportunity, not only of

getting fit themselves but also of riding in each other's company. Then I should arrange to transport the team to the scene of the race in time to allow plenty of opportunity for thorough acclimatisation. Massage and full training facilities would be available and I think that a British team might then have a reasonable chance of success in any international race on foreign roads. "

His experiences in the Olympic Games were obviously still on his mind. Throughout the interview Charles emphasised that his views were not infallible, as he was aware of the pitfalls of gener-alisations, and regarding training in particular, he thought that 'every man must stick to the methods which he knows are suited to himself'.

Each year in March all the races that were approved for the Best All-Rounder (BAR) were published. With seventy-six 50-mile races, thirty-one 100-mile and twenty-one 12-hour events spread all over the country, the popularity of cycle racing in Britain at this time is in no doubt. In 1932 *Cycling* magazine broke its circulation record, since it was first published in 1891, with 64,762 copies sold in April. The crowds that actually cycled to see road races were described by the magazine as 'getting out of hand' and 'events in the country that were never previously troubled with congestion are now seriously embarrassed by it'.

Against this exciting background, the 1933 racing season began well for Charles with a win in the Crescent Wheelers '25' followed by a win in the MC&AC '50' and '25' as well as the Warwickshire Road '50'.

June saw the World's Cycling Championship Trial at Brooklands, the famous motor racing track at Weybridge, Surrey. The previous year A. R. M. Harbour, A. V. Jenner and W. J. Mills had ridden in the World's Championship in Rome and on their return they had decided that it was essential for British riders to train for such events. The Brooklands race was the result of their efforts to provide this type of training. It would give British cyclists experience of continental massed-start racing, which was so different to the time trials that they were used to, and would encourage team racing. Not since 1922 when David Marsh took the World's Cycling Road Championship, had a British rider won an International road race.

The afternoon's events started with an appearance by Oliver Bertram in his record breaking Delange 12-cylinder car. A three-lap motorcycle handicap race should have been the next event but this was cancelled due to heavy rain and the danger of skidding at high speed. A thrilling demonstration flight by a Hawker Hart aeroplane followed. At 4.00 p.m., the big event, the 100-kilometre massed-start trial, was started by Sir Malcolm Cambell MBE (father of Donald Cambell), the land speed record holder of the time. Ninety-one cyclists started the 17-lap course; every third lap included Test Hill with a gradient of 1:4 at the top. Only fourteen riders finished the race. Thrills and spills were the order of the day, with 55 race *primes* (intermediate sprints with bonuses) introduced to make the race more exciting. Charles, riding with S. T. Parker and H. Sutton, in dark blue shirts, were the MC&AC team. The race was a disappointment for Charles who smashed his wheel early on and retired. It was won by J. J. Salt (Liverpool District) with W. F. Burl, (Marlborough) second and H. Sutton (MC&AC) third in a very close finish. Burl, who we hear more of later, was the only rider to have ridden up Test Hill on all five occasions.

It was in September that Charles did his best ride of 1933 in the Manchester Wheelers 12-hour race. He rode a remarkable total of 238¼ miles breaking the previous record set by J. Lauterwasser of 237⅞ miles in 1928. He maintained a regular pace of 20 mph

throughout the day and towards the end showed every likelihood of keeping to that speed, or even increasing it to 22 mph. Then came a piece of really bad luck, a puncture which put paid to his attempt to cover over 240 miles.

This year Frank Southall won the Best All-Rounder competition for the fourth year in succession – the only winner since its inauguration. His best average speed for a '50' a '100' and a 12-hour was 21.731 mph. S. M. Butler was second with 21.443 mph and Charles third with 21.439 mph.

In May 1934, for a second time, Charles won the Anfield '100' in 4 hr. 41 min. 8 sec. a record for the course. This was followed by another big win in the Highgate '100'. Headlined as 'Holland's Smashing Win' his time of 4 hr. 33 min. 31 sec. was a course record, a personal record, a club record and the fastest '100' of the year. The dramatic account of the race in *Cycling* read:

A fast car speeds down the narrow lane to the cluster of people at the end. A man jumps out and hurries across to the timekeeper by the side of the grass verge. News of the race: 'James caught Butler at 85 miles and is scrapping with him, but Holland is moving like the wind and looks likely to catch them both.'

An excited buzz runs through the crowd, James caught Butler who started seven minutes in front! And Holland moving like the wind had started fourteen minutes behind Butler! 'Man-up', the crowd is on tip toe. Someone shouts, 'it's Holland', but it can't be; what's happened to James and Butler? There is no time for argument, for a split-second later Holland, the dusky, smiling Midlander flashes over the line.

Shortly after this event in June 1934, the team to represent England in the World's Road Racing Championship to be held in Leipzig on 18 August, was announced. F. C. Ghilks, P. T. Stallard,

F. C. Ghilks, C. Holland and P. Stallard at the start of the amateur race in the World Road Racing Championship in Leipzig, Germany in 1934.

W. G. Barnes (reserve) and C. Holland were to travel to Germany to ride in the amateur road race. The course was nearly six-miles which the competitors had to cover twelve times. The roads were closed, lamp-posts removed, corners were banked and the marshalling was done by Leipzig brownshirts (the Nazi paramilitary). The event was ridden at the tremendous average speed of 26 mph and one lap of 6 miles was covered at nearly 30 mph.

Charles rode splendidly, cornering superbly and as the best unpaced stayer in the field he might well have won with a solo ride at the front of the bunch, but for the fact that he rode 60 of the 70 miles with three broken spokes. He was using light alloy metal sprint rims and, as a result, the wheel immediately went out of true, touching the forks on both sides and rubbing away the fabric walls of the tyre. A wobbly front wheel made high speed cornering difficult and a complete collapse of the wheel was always imminent. In 'Our Modest Champion', *The Roll Call* reported: 'Whether our imperturbable Charles was upset by this fact nobody knows and he won't tell you.' What he did say was that he thought the race was carried out in the fairest and cleanest possible spirit: the German officials made all their visitors exceedingly welcome and did everything possible for their comfort. The event was won by Kees Pellenaars (Holland), André Deforge (France) was second, and Paul André (Belgium) was third. Charles came in fourth but, almost six months later, this was changed to third as André was disqualified on the question of amateur status. Stallard and Ghilks had trouble-free rides with Stallard finishing seventh. Thirty-six riders representing thirteen nations started and twenty-six finished.

Referring to Charles' ride, *Cycling* reported: 'Class told, and this country's face was saved, to an extent by the fact that the England selectors had in one case out of the four selections, ignored the Brooklands' results and chosen a man whom, all the country had known for two years, had the class necessary to remain with the leaders'. Kaers from Belgium won the professional road event, and in a thrilling final, in front of a home crowd of thousands, Metz came in first in the motor-paced championship.

On his return from Germany, Charles once again had his sights set on the BAR. There was one 12-hour event which he could enter to get a good ride in, that of the Manchester Wheelers, which he had won in the previous year. He needed to equal or near equal that record-breaking ride, as E. J. Capell had already ridden 236 miles in a 12-hour. Although it was considered to be attainable, Charles only managed about 232 miles and this was not enough to keep him at the top of the tables. Capell held on to his lead and won the BAR with an average speed of 21.622 mph. Charles was second and H. James third.

On 28 January 1935, 7,000 people from all over the British Isles attended the Best All-Rounder Prize Giving and Concert held in the Albert Hall, London. The atmosphere at these events was very special, they had a certain 'something … a feeling, that cannot be described that makes this gathering of the nation's wheelfolk unique. I can define it only as being the spirit that is always so naturally and closely associated with the bicycle and the greatest of all games, cycling!', so said *Cycling*.

The concert prior to the prize giving was a complete mixture of 'turns', popular tunes played on an organ, the Coldstream Guards, the eight Rodney Hudson Dancing Girls, the seven Thunderbolts, described as whirling Arabian acrobats, and the three Accordian Kings. This was followed by a home trainer competition (cycling on rollers) and then burlesque dancers, 'Wilson, Keppell and Betty, entertained in a seriously side-splitting manner'.

The presentations followed. Roland E. Dangerfield, Managing Director of Temple Press Ltd., the proprietors of *Cycling*, and the Chairman of the Fifth BAR said of Charles:

Charles Holland was third in 1933 and in 1934 he is second. Many of us expected him to be first. He was in fact, quite an obvious choice, on what we had all seen. And very early in the season Holland, who finished up 1933 with a competition record at 12-hours, began winning 50-mile events with ease and regularity. At 100 miles we knew he was a 'smasher'. Here, then was surely the 'Best All-Rounder' ready made! Once again, however, we saw how true it is that 'there's many a slip'. Holland, after a disappointment in the Bath Road '100' earlier in the year went abroad for the World's Championship, put up a splendid sprinting effort therein, then came back and, hard as he tried, he was never again quite the Holland we had known earlier in the year. He required to do a 12-hour that ought to have been well within his powers but that figure just eluded him. Hard luck Holland.

Those who had ridden to the event collected their cycles from the cellars of the Albert Hall before making their way into the cold night air.

Later that year in May, Charles had two good 50-mile wins in the Charlotteville and Notts Castle events, and these were followed by a surprising victory at the seventh annual Bournville sports day.

Taken in 1935, this shows Charles at the start of the Polytechnic 12-hour time trial. The official makes a note of his exact start time.

Charles showed a great burst of speed and wonderful track craft to win the 500-yard scratch race for the Brooks Bowl. The following day he did 2 hr. 14 min. 54 sec. in the Liverpool '50', showing his versatility on a bike.

Nevertheless, not every event bought success. 'Mere novices' was how the English team were described after competing in an amateur race between five nations at the Tuileries Gardens, Paris, in June. The race was 100 kilometres (62 miles) and the circuit 1.25 kilometre (¾ mile) to be covered 80 times, the corners were right angles and the surface was loose gravel. P. T. Stallard, E. V. Mills and W. Harvell went down in the first lap. Stallard crashed four times in total and smashed his bike up. Charles managed to remain upright, but had to retire halfway through as he was suffering from a pain in his side. Mills and Harvell were placed in a group coming eleventh. Somewhat disparagingly, it was noted by the MC&AC that Charles' absence at the Anfield '100' held at the same time, was because he was 'a man who knows his own mind best and that if he prefers the gardens of the Tuileries to the battleground of Shropshire there is no more to be said'.

The next major event, in the cycling calendar was the World's Cycling Championship held at Donnington Park, Leicestershire at the end of June. R. Charpentier, J. Goujon, and R. Mauret were the first three respectively to finish, a grand-slam for France. Charles was the first of the English riders to finish – 12 minutes behind the winner and with a six-length lead over W. G. Barnes who was fourth. Again, the British press told it like it was. *Cycling* reported: 'The Donnington Trial was not a race it was a lesson. If the people concerned learn from it, then it will have served a purpose; otherwise it remains a disgraceful fiasco, so far as this country's part in it is concerned, and the most damming commentary upon our ambitions to play the game in massed-start racing.'

One of the main problems was that the English riders failed to ride as a team. This was partly due to the fact it was a selection race and there was rivalry between the riders. The French riders showed staying, sprinting and hill-climbing qualities and the ability to take food and drink on board with no loss of speed and, most importantly, they rode as a team. Lapébie the fourth member of the French team changed his tyre following a puncture and only lost just over two minutes but he retired when he punctured again.

In July 1935 Charles, along with Nievergelt from Switzerland and Wolkert from Germany, was invited by the Danish cycling Union to take part in their Star Race in Roskilde. The cycling press believed that a Dane would win and that Frode Sorenson, Werner Grundahl-Hansen, Knud Jacobsen and Leo Nielsen were a quartet considered to be the best in Europe. When asked in a Danish press interview before the race whether he was in good form Charles replied, 'I was before leaving home but the sea was a little rough last night and this morning.' 'Are you the best amateur in England?', to which Charles replied, 'I suppose so now Southall has turned professional.' He declined to comment on his chances in the race but admitted no prior knowledge of it, except that Southall had told him that it was a difficult race for a foreigner to win. This proved to be the case and Charles was unplaced and once again disappointed.

On his return from Denmark, Charles, P. Stallard and L. Youll were selected to represent England in the World's Championships in Belgium. This time the press were full of praise for Charles: 'If we had three Hollands our chance of winning a championship would be something to bet on.' The week after reports continued in the same vein. 'The only rider with any pretensions to massed-start racing ability, C. Holland, who was the first choice for our World's Championship, may not represent England after all. It has

In 1935, Charles went to Copenhagen to take part in the famous Star international event. Here, he is seen checking his gear before going on a training run.

been announced on Holland's behalf business engagements will keep him at home during August.'

In September 1935 it was once more the Manchester Wheelers 12-hour event, which proved to be a good race for two of the Holland brothers and the MC&AC. The weather conditions were dreadful, Charles had four punctures and lost touch with the helpers, which meant that he missed food and drinks. Undaunted, he made a magnificent effort and covered 236½ miles – the winning distance. His brother Alfred, riding in his second 12-hour, supported Charles in true brotherly style and covered 219 miles,

The end of the Manchester Wheelers 12-hour race in 1935. Charles won, supported by his brother Alf (left) and the MC&AC received the team prize.

even though he had five punctures! The third MC&AC rider, A. Clark, did 209 miles, which meant that they won the team prize as well.

Another year almost over and another BAR competition coming to a close. Charles, who left it rather late to attack the BAR times, needed a very good ride in the last qualifying race of the season, the Rugby '50'. A time of 2 hr. 8 min. 25 sec. would put him in first place, ahead of S. W. Miles. The situation was tense, Miles who had already finished stood watching. The crowd waited in anticipation, and with an almost super-human effort Charles crossed the finish line. Then came the calm, unhurried timekeeper's announce-ment, '2 hr. 8 min. 25.6 sec.'. Charles had won the race but three-fifths of a second meant that Miles had won the BAR. Another failure, when the calculations were com-plete he was beaten by one thousandth of a mile per hour, so it was second again for Charles. Frank Lipscombe came third.

In the following January the Albert Hall was packed for the ceremony to award the prizes for this event. The same eclectic mix

of entertainment was provided, with Larry Adler, the harmonica player, the star of the show. The celebrities chatted with the club riders, some women wore shorts and others evening dress, the crowd cheered the winners, and at the end of the evening everyone joined hands to sing 'Auld Lang Syne'. It seems that it was another successful celebration of a cycling year.

Charles was never a professional for Hercules but did work for them as a representative.

CHAPTER 5

Holland for England

At the start of this Olympic year no one in cycling, or in any other sport for that matter, had given any thought to the fact that the next Games wouldn't be in another four years, but in another twelve years in 1948, after the Second World War.

Prior to the start of the racing season the cycling press had plenty of time to speculate on the year ahead and Charles certainly had his share of the copy. On 1 January *Cycling* magazine talked of him as being a possible selection for the Olympics, and in April their thoughts had already turned to the BAR and of Charles said: 'No one can doubt that Holland has the ability to bring the BAR, average to 22 mph. The question is whether he wants to do it. If international racing claims his attention his serious English season will begin in August and he must know what that means.'

The MC&AC pursued a similar line of thought and believed that he could be supreme as a sprinter or a long distance road man if he specialised in either discipline. However, their main interest was in the Holland brothers and whether the eldest brother Walter could get fit again so that the four brothers could ride as a team. Walter had actually retired from racing before the youngest brother Jack started entering events, but in June 1936 they all raced against each other in a club '30'. The expected duel between Charles and Alf ended in favour of the latter by 28 seconds. Jack finished a couple of minutes slower as did Walter who it seemed was dissatisfied with his come-back time. Nonetheless, 1936 was to be the year that Alf and Jack, the two younger brothers, came into their own. *The Roll Call* enjoyed comments such as, 'Alf Holland! Some lad! Charles the First will have to look to his laurels. We now know what made the yellow triplet go so swiftly.' The triplet referred to, also known as the 'yellow peril' was ridden at tremendous speed once all three brothers were on board.

Alf went on to win both the Crescent Wheelers and the Leicester Roads open 25-mile races. In the MC&AC's first '50' of the season

Alf Holland being steadied by Frank Greenwood at the start of the Leicester Roads open 25-mile race, which he went on to win.

in April, Alf beat Charles and in May went one better when he broke Charles' course record with a winning time of 2 hr. 14 min. 8 sec. Jack was also racing now and competed well in both the Warwick and the Notts Castle Open races along with his brothers.

In addition to local club events there were two Olympic trial massed-start races at around this time. The first, a 25-mile event, was held at the Birchfield Harriers track in Birmingham. Twenty riders took part and their times were slower than those they would normally achieve on the road. After 12 miles the event developed into a procession, with Alf taking the lead and lapping his rivals, including his brother, who gave him a great deal of assistance once a lap separated them. The final placings were Alf first and Charles second.

The Holland brothers, Charles, Jack and Alf, on the 'yellow peril' – a bicycle made for three – all wearing their Sunday-best cycling gear.

Charles gained his revenge in the next race in May at Donington Park, Leicestershire. Held in driving rain and a strong wind, over 100 km (62 miles), only 11 of the 60 starters finished. No teams were entered on purpose so that individual effort could be observed. As a result, slower riders sat on the fastest men's wheels throughout the race, but each lap took its toll. Charles, recognised as the best man in England at massed-start racing, won in 2 hrs. 44 min. 22.6 sec. A. Bevan finished a length behind him followed by E. Larkin. Alf finished in a group of four in fourth place.

The Cyclist magazine reported on the event in scathing terms:

It is hard to see what else the selectors, have gleaned of value from the event commensurate with all the trouble, time and expense involved on such a miserable day (apart from the fact that Charles would be fairly certain of Olympic selection!). Everybody was soaked to the skin, the men finished in a state unrecognisable as that of human beings. The fact that many of the likeliest candidates for Olympic selection were absent emphasises the inconclusive nature of the race as a useful trial.

It is noteworthy that in an article written well before this trial the great Frank Southall had argued:

I am of the opinion that the Brooklands and Donington Park trials are absolute washouts unless the chosen team (and second-choice team, for comparison purposes) ride together as a team and not as individuals. By all means have such trials, but select a team, not necessarily the final choice, and pit it against all the other riders also riding as teams.

A certain amount of controversy was brewing with regard to the procedures for Olympic selection, just as it had in 1932.

At the end of May on the Whit Monday bank holiday, it was once again the annual Anfield '100'. It attracted 190 entrants and up to this point in time was classed as the greatest ever held. Charles thought that his performance in this event was his best effort of 1936, and it is described here in his own words, starting with the preparation for the race.

"We started training more conscientiously, going to bed earlier, doing longer training rides, and endeavouring to be as fit as possible for what some consider to be the hardest race at the distance. One particular training ride stands out very clearly in my memory. A week before the event on the Sunday Alf and I set out for Salop, doing a bit-and-bit into a strong headwind, and then we battled around the Anfield course. We had fought it out for about 100 miles, both of us feeling a little worse for wear, so we contemplated a quiet ride home. It was not to be, however; a club mate was waiting for us about 20 miles from home, no doubt with the intention of giving us a hiding, and those last few miles along the Watling Street just about finished us. Still, with one or two shorter rides during the week we faced the timekeeper on the Whit-Monday with every confidence.

I rode at a fairly even speed throughout the race; it was very cold at the beginning of the race but was much warmer towards the end. The aches one usually gets when one keeps trying to go faster and faster were forgotten on seeing the vast crowds who annually make the Anfield course their Mecca on Whit Monday. My actual time for the event was 4 hr. 33 min. 29 sec. Alf was second fastest, 11 minutes slower, but he was unfortunate to puncture, and also had trouble, losing the spring off his derailleur gear. As it was, his improved performance gave him the first handicap award and I took second handicap from scratch, as I was conceding 15 minutes to him. Our third man, Syd Middleton crashed when doing the ride of his life and was unable to finish much to his disappointment. If an MC&AC rider had finished in less than 5½ hours, it would have meant the team prize as well.

Although my time for this event is almost 7 minutes slower than when I broke the competition record in the Leamington '100', the difference in the courses accounts for this, as riders who have competed on the undulating roads of Shropshire will testify.

A lot of the credit for our success goes to the army of helpers who were down the road at the exact spot they were asked to be, handing out the correct drink and diligently following the instructions given to them. I am fortunate in having plenty of helpers and I could not wish for a better organiser than my eldest brother Walter, who has retired from racing but acts as manager on these occasions.

The amusing part about the Anfield ride was that I left the finish resigned to second fastest time, as one rider had already been clocked in doing a ride two minutes faster than mine. Most members of the MC&AC present agreed with me on the possibility of such a ride; but Frank Urry was most insistent on its impossibility, because the rider was too much in arrears at 80 miles to have beaten my record for the course.

It was several hours later when I learned that Frank, whose leg had been pulled unmercifully by the other members for being so obstinate, was right. The other rider had inadvertently taken a short route, and so my best ride ended first in elation, then in disappointment, followed by uncertainty and finally jubilation. 🙶🙶

It was disappointing for Charles and Alf that Jack wasn't riding with them. Their father had refused to give permission for him to ride as he thought 100 miles too far for a youngster. Instead, and rather ironically, Jack went to a grass track meeting, won a clock and rode home afterwards – well over 100 miles in total.

June certainly was a busy cycling month for Charles and his two younger brothers. The Olympic team had not yet been announced and one can only speculate that with this in mind some of the races were ridden the way they were. The East Liverpool Wheelers '50' at the beginning of June was won by H. James, with B. W. Bentley second and Alf third. Charles, who thought that he had let the side down, came in sixth and Jack with an allowance of 7½ minutes easily won the handicap award. The Hollands took second place in the team shield.

A few days later on Thursday 18 June, Charles took part in the thrills and spills of the first massed-start race around the gruelling motorbike Tourist Trophy course on the Isle of Man. The race (organised by the Viking Wheelers Cycling Club), over 37½ miles, aroused a great deal of enthusiasm. Eighty-one riders started and great crowds lined the roads and altogether it was hugely successful. At the start, one great splash of vivid colours in the blazing sun, the announcer warned the riders: 'This is not to be one glorious "blind" like the TT You are expected to observe the ordinary traffic rules of the road and you may meet on-coming traffic, so be careful.' The cyclists seemed to ignore this warning altogether! An Act, which covered the closure of roads for the motorbikes, did not cover the cyclists and, although most people kept off the road, a few local motorcyclists caused a bit of a nuisance.

Three *primes* were awarded during the race. Charles won the first for a severe hill-climbing test on Creg Wylley. J. Holmes of Yorkshire Road Club won the second for the first arrival at Ramsey. W. Messer of Marlborough Road Club, who arrived first at the Bungalow, won the third.

At the finishing line people craned their necks to get a glimpse of the riders with excitement at fever pitch. 'What a race, what a course and what a finish!' *The Bicycle* reported:

June 24, 1936.

£71

𝔊𝔜𝔠𝔩𝔦𝔫𝔤

ISLE OF MAN RACE PHOTO NEWS

Caught by Cycling cameras during the Isle of Man massed-start race (full report on pages 864-865). C. Holland (2), winner, with cup, W. Messer (5), second, and J. G. Bone (6), third. (1) The leaders cornering at Craig-ny-Baa. (3) Round the hairpin at Governor's Bridge. (4) A rider who could not quite get round. (7) Harvell hits the sandbags. (8) Another fails to corner properly. (9) First spill down Bray Hill. (10) "Got him!" (11) The beginning of the mountain climb.

A27

Three riders were fighting every inch of the way with the crowd cheering itself hoarse. Over the finishing line they flashed. A yard between first and second, only five yards between second and third! Who had won? Few could tell for the numbers were not easily discernible with the riders bent low over their machines. Then came the official announcement; first C. Holland, 1 hr. 42 min. 57 sec., second W. Messer, 1 hr. 42 min. 58 sec. and third J. G. Bone, 1 hour 42 min. 59 sec.

E. S. Orbell who rode the last ten miles alone came in a good fourth. There had been many crashes during the race resulting in minor injuries; two cyclists broke their collarbones and six other people needed hospital treatment. Only 48 riders finished the race. Part of *Cycling's* report read:

Three hours before the bicycle race began a dozen of the greatest motorcyclists in the country had risked death hurtling round this tortuous course at speeds exceeding 100 mph. These men of iron nerve, with a roaring, vibrating engine between their knees, swept down the mountain road their machines at times leaving the road altogether. Yet so spectacular was the sight of cyclists flat out down the same road that even the most experienced driver was thrilled. One famous TT winner told us afterwards he would never have the nerve to take Craig-ny-Baa corner at the speed that Holland sped round!

The first massed-start race on the Isle of Man TT course would be remembered for years by those who watched it and, naturally, by those who took part in it. Not only was it remembered by Charles but also revisited by him many years later.

The next important event in this hectic month was the final Olympic team selection trial held at Donington on 21 June.

A relatively unknown cyclist, J. Fancourt of Yorkshire Road Club, won, beating the fancied men and putting the selectors in a quandary. Fancourt had fallen and retired in the previous Donington trial and the Isle of Man race. Only 16 out of a field of 101 finished and 40 riders were treated by ambulance men. The final stages of the race were best described in *The Bicycle*:

Nobody wanted to go. A mile to go and still no effort. Half a mile still calm prevailed. Four hundred yards to go, Charlie Holland is away! On his wheel was Stallard with the field a little way back. Then Holland looked round and slowed. He was looking for his brother Alf, anxious to have him on his wheel and make certain of a place for him. And in that split second when Holland eased, Fancourt saw his chance and took it. He went through like a flash and was in the lead. Only a few yards to go, Holland was straining every effort to get level but it was too late. Fancourt sped over the line in 2 hr. 46 min. 11.8 sec.

Charles was second and P. T. Stallard third. Alf finished in a group classed as fifth and Jack, who also finished, was a lap behind. He had stayed behind with Charles when he had had trouble with his chain so that they could work together to catch the field, but then Jack had puncture troubles of his own.

Nevertheless, in *Cycling*, 24 June, the heading in the 'Our points of View' feature read: 'Holland for England' and went on to say:

With C. Holland as No.1 choice for England, might not his chances be enhanced if his backers were the closest teamsters of all – his own brothers? After all, the selection of C. Holland 'to win' for England needs no committee decision. Their task to pick the men who will do all they can to make that achievement possible even to the point of

The Holland brothers (Charles, Alf and Jack) raced with each other on numerous occasions but, unfortunately, were not selected to ride as a team in the Berlin Olympic Games. Once again Frank Greenwood and Walter are there to support them.

sinking their own individuality. England's Holland team! There is at least a thought in it worthy of consideration psychologically as well as from an individual merit point of view. If the last Donington trial had been teamed more thoughtfully, with perhaps this family idea tried out, we might have learned a good deal more than we know now.

Had Charles read the above report when, at the beginning of July, the National 25-mile Championship took place at the Butts Ground, Coventry. It would appear so, because a headline read, 'Massed-Start Tactics by Holland Family Disturb the Sprinters'. The article on the race continued, 'There was a team entered, it was composed of the three brothers Holland and the youngest of them, Jack is now the title holder.' In one of the most exciting races of its kind, Jack at 19, probably the youngest to ever hold the title, rode a remarkable race winning by a wheel. The brothers had done their best for each other, with ten laps to go Charles retired and Alf came in one of the five official finishers. F. C. Ghilks was second and L. Youll third. At the end of the race the delight on the faces of the brothers said it all! It was thought at this time that Alf and Jack would keep the Holland name to the forefront in cycling for the next decade. How little people knew of what lay ahead.

Not long after this event, but after months of trials and meetings, the Berlin Olympic Cycling Team was finally announced

The British cycling team: back row, officials; second row, from left to right, E. A. Johnson, J. G. Bone, R. Hicks, H. H. Hill, A. Bevan; front row, from left to right, H. N. Crowe, W. T. Hall, E. H. Chambers, J. E. Sibbit, C. T. King, W. A. Messer, C. Holland.

(see page 98). Charles was selected to ride in the 100-kilometre massed-start road race and was to be a reserve for the 4,000-metre team pursuit. As always much was written about the selection including *Cycling's*, gloomy prediction, 'Unfortunately, it must be stated that if these are our best men then they are unlikely to bring back any Olympic titles from Germany.'

The International Olympic Committee (IOC) had awarded the Games to Berlin in 1931 with no idea that Adolph Hitler would take power in Germany two years later. By 1936 the Nazis had control and had already begun to implement their racist policies. Many countries particularly the United States proposed a boycott of the Games and an alternative event called the People's Games was being planned for Barcelona. The outbreak of the Spanish Civil War destroyed this idea and the Spanish, who withdrew because of this, were in the end, the only notable absentees. The German IOC and the German Reich had repeatedly given assurances that they would abide by the rules of Olympic competition. These pledges, together with the smooth running of the Winter Games held at Garmisch-Partenkichen in Germany earlier in the year, ensured that the Games would go ahead.

The then president of the IOC, Count de Baillet-Latour made an interesting point at the end of his invitation to the competitors:

Berlin invites the sporting youth to the Festival of the Eleventh Olympic Games and it is hoped that this invitation will be accepted throughout the world. We are convinced that magnificent contests will take place when strength and ability are matched. We hope, however, that the Games will have a deeper significance than this and that from this international festival a strong, mutual understanding will develop and that these peaceful competitions will lead to permanent friendships that will serve the cause of peace.

Chancellor Adolph Hitler seized on this opportunity to show the efficiency and might of his regime. Large stadiums, swimming pools, an outdoor theatre, a polo field and an Olympic village with 150 houses for the male athletes were specially built. Each house accommodated about 25 men who slept two to a room. In addition each building had washrooms and showers, a common room facing a terrace, a telephone booth, a steward's room, a refrigerator and storage facilities in the attic.

In the village itself many excellent facilities were provided for the competitors, such as dining rooms where teams could take their own chefs. There were banks, post offices, newspaper stands,

The Berlin Olympic village accommodated 6,000 competitors and officials. The crescent-shaped building on the left housed the reception and administration headquarters, including the press office, a post office and a bank.

barbers, laundries, as well as shops selling sports goods, stationary, photographic equipment, fruit and confectionary. Special entertainment was provided and services were arranged for every religion. Saunas, Finnish vapour baths, medicinal baths and, much to Charles' relief, masseurs were all available.

On the down side visitors were strictly controlled and no women at all were allowed to enter the village. And at ten o'clock each night the lights went out – it was curfew hour!

The female competitors were housed in what was called the Women's Dormitory – a three-storey building situated at the northern end of the Reich Sports Field (Reichsportfeld). Like the men they slept two to a room (not really a dormitory), but their facilities differed in that they had a sewing room and a hairdressers in the basement with 'cosmetics of every kind to hand'. The Dormitory was to be used by students of the Reich Academy of Physical Culture after the Games.

There were many technological achievements at the Berlin Games. Events were televised for the first time on a closed circuit system and shown throughout the Olympic village and on screens set up around the country. Zeppelins carried newsreel film to other European cities, and results were transmitted to news media by telex as soon as events were completed.

In addition, the first official film of events, *Olympia* by Leni Riefenstal, was produced. Although it was originally intended as Nazi propaganda, *Olympia* is a highly respected cinematic work, which not only documents the Games but also celebrates the human spirit.

Perhaps because the Games were being held in Europe or perhaps because of politics, the British cycling team departed for Germany on 30 July from Liverpool Street Station, London with less publicity than for the previous Olympics. Charles, whose views were usually published in long interviews and articles said and wrote surprisingly little about these games. The nationalistic and militaristic atmosphere alarmed many of the athletes and the press. Swastikas, portraits of Hitler, flags as well as flowers decorated Berlin and martial music blared out through loud speakers. Some journalists suspected that their rooms had been searched and that letters and articles were subject to censorship.

The grand opening ceremony was run with military precision on the afternoon of 1 August. A fleet of buses ferried the athletes from the Olympic village to the Reichsportfeld. The record-breaking Hindenberg airship, with swastikas on its tail fin and towing an Olympic flag cruised overhead. Huge crowds packed the streets of Berlin hoping to catch a glimpse of Chancellor Adolph Hitler, standing, in uniform, in the front of an open car, on his way to the stadium. The noise as he entered was deafening. The spectators cheered and fanfares blared out. Once he and his entourage, which included Hess and Goebbels, were seated the flags of the 52 nations taking part were ceremoniously raised, whilst for the first time in Olympic history, a huge bell tolled. Around the bell were the words *Ich rufe die Jugend der Welt*, meaning, 'I call the youth of the world'.

Next, to an uproarious welcome, in marched the teams in alphabetical order. When the German team entered almost the whole stadium were on their feet and 100,000 arms were raised in salute. The British team, led by the rower Jack Beresford making his fifth Olympic appearance did an 'eyes right' in lieu of a salute and the Americans removed their boaters and placed them on their chests. With all the teams assembled a recording of the Olympic Creed by Baron de Coubertin was broadcast. As the Olympic flag was raised Hitler declared the Games of the eleventh Olympiad of the modern era open and 20,000 pigeons were released.

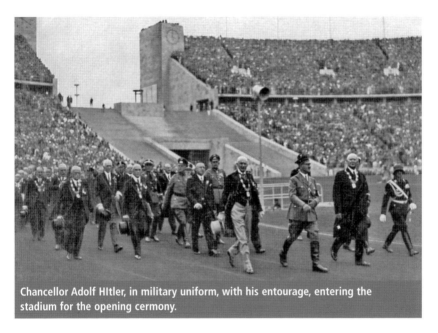

Chancellor Adolf HItler, in military uniform, with his entourage, entering the stadium for the opening cermony.

Richard Strauss conducted his own Olympic hymn and as it faded away silence fell as a torch bearer entered the stadium to light the Olympic flame. At the suggestion of Carl Diem, chairman of the organising committee, the torch had been lit for the first time in Olympia, Greece and more than 3,000 runners had carried it to Berlin. The choir, dressed in white, sang the *Hallelujah Chorus*. The Olympic Oath: 'In the name of all the competitors, I promise that we shall take part in these Olympic Games, respecting and abiding by the rules that govern them, in the true spirit of sportsmanship, for the glory of sport and the honour of our teams', was taken by the German weightlifter, Rudolf Ismayr, the Los Angeles Olympic champion, prior to the teams leaving the stadium.

In the evening in the magnificently lit stadium there were gymnastics, singing and dancing by thousands of well-drilled children taking part in what was called a Festival Play entitled 'Olympic

Youth'. A procession of flags accompanied the orchestra as they played Verdi's *Grand March* from *Aida*. This ceremony ended with searchlights lighting up the night sky and a choir of 1,500 joining in Beethoven's Choral Symphony. The stage was set for the historical sporting events to follow.

On his arrival in Berlin the editor of *Cycling* had great difficulty in finding the cycle track in Charlottenburg, which he put down to the general lack of interest shown by the German authorities in cycling. Originally, it was decided that the cycling events would be run in the old Berlin velodrome, then plans were made for a new cement track and finally, as this was too costly, a 400-metre wooden bowl was set down on the football pitch of the Berlin Sports Club close to the Avus Motor Track.

Charles' event began at 8.00 a.m. on the bright sunny morning of 8 August. Starting on the Avus Motor Track on the outskirts of Berlin, the course went over the narrow roads of the Forest of Grunewald and then back to the track for the finish. All the spectators and officials waited in the grandstand while loudspeakers announced the progress of the riders. The 100-kilometre road race was to be a massed start for the first time in Olympic history. Although a comparatively slow race – the English team did better times in training – it was extremely dangerous. Sixty riders were in the leading bunch at 81 km and nearly thirty at 91 km. The surface varied from cobbles to loose sand and the lane leading into the Avus track was only three yards wide. The course was criticised, as it contained no long or steep hills, making a breakaway impossible. Not a single rider was dropped for lack of speed.

The English team were reported as riding splendidly although their names were never mentioned in the bulletins from the course, either as leaders or for being dropped. Only towards the end did they, amid great excitement from the English camp, come into the

Cyclists at the beginning of the 100-km massed-start race leaving the Berlin Sports Club near to the Avus Motor Track.

OLYMPIC GAMES 1936
THE BRITISH CYCLING TEAM

1, C. Holland (road race); 2, J. G. Bone (road race); 3, D. T. Blick (reserve, 1,000 metres time trial and for team pursuit final selection); 4, A. N. Holland (reserve, road race); 5, C. T. King (for team pursuit final selection); 6, A. Bevan (road race); 7, W. A. Messer (road race); 8, H. H. Hill (for team pursuit final selection); 9, E. V. Mills (for team pursuit final selection and road race reserve); 10, R. Hicks (1,000 metres time trial and sprint race); 11, E. A. Johnson (for team pursuit final selection); 12, J. E. Siblit and E. H. Chambers (tandem race).

news, when it was announced there were three English riders in the first five. Three hundred metres from the line Charles had the lead, but it did not last, and Robert Charpentier of France came in first in 2 hr. 33 min. 05 sec., followed by Guy Lapébie also of France in 2 hr. 33 min. 05.2 sec., and then Ernst Nievergelt from Switzerland in 2 hr. 33 min. 05.8 sec. Charles finished in a bunch of five riders in 2 hr. 33 min. 06 sec., Fritz Scheller of Germany just beat him on the line in the same time. It is reported that Lapébie inexplicably slowed down almost at the line. A photograph is said to show Charpentier pulling his rival back by his shirt!

The Roll Call summarised the event:

It must have been a nightmare kind of event and one in which only the strongest combinations could have kept a rider in the front bunch. Charlie could not gather his compatriots round him and from what we can understand he had to fight his way, elbowing, jostling and pushing to occupy a front position in that fierce affair. Very many riders came to grief, a happening that overtook most of the other British representatives; but Charlie sailed through barging and bucking into the excited crowd and actually leading the field a few hundred yards from the finishing tape.

Of the other British riders, Messer, with just 3 km to go was run into and his wheel was stripped of spokes and, almost at the finish, Bevan was touched by a Dutch rider and both came down. He walked his bike across the line and was later taken to hospital. Fortunately, his injuries were not severe. In the last mile J. G. Bone, who had supported Charles well, was brought off twice. The first time he remounted quickly and caught the field but after the second fall he was alone and finished well back. The French won the team race. This was the largest Olympic road race field ever, with 100 entries from 29 nations – some riders were still finishing 15 minutes after the winner.

In the tandem race J. E. Sibbit and E. H. Chambers were beaten in the third heat by their old rivals B. Leene and H. Ooms of Holland, and R. Hicks finished seventh in the 1-km time trial.

As always, there were events that caused controversy. In the 4,000-metre team pursuit, according to the programme, the semi-final winners went into the final, and the fastest losers would automatically be third. The semi-final times were France 4 min. 2 sec., Italy 4 min. 49 sec., Britain 4 min. 50 sec., and Germany 4 min. 54 sec. However, a sudden decision was made to race the British and German teams. By staging this match for the losers, Germany had another chance for a place. The British win was, therefore, even more satisfactory. The French team of R. Charpentier, G. Lapébie, J. Goujon and R. J. Le Nizhery riding superbly, as had been expected, won overall.

The other cycling controversy was in the sprint final. Some observers thought that Toni Merkens of Germany fouled Arie Van Vliet Long of Holland who finished second. The German should have been disqualified but instead was fined 100 marks. There were no German or Dutch officials involved in this decision and this probably prevented a riot by spectators.

The racing reporters of the day all agreed that in the five races the five best men or team had won. Charpentier won three gold medals and Lapébie won two golds and a silver. In addition to their medals, all winners were presented with small potted oak trees for replanting in their 'homeland'.

It is interesting to note that travelling with the British cycling team were two masseurs. One of the two, W. T. Hall, was classed as a 'masseur-mechanic'. Obviously a man good with his hands!

Despite the preliminary doubts about holding the Games in

Germany, the leaders of the Third Reich did everything they could to make the Games a success and they welcomed more athletes (4,069 of whom only 328 were women) from more countries (49) than any previous Olympics to compete in 129 events. The host nation topped the medal table with 89 including 33 gold (this was partly due to the expanded number of men's gymnastic events).

The most popular hero of the games was Jesse Owens, the African American, who won four gold medals. Much has been written about Hitler refusing to congratulate Jesse Owens. It seems, however, that on the first day he was told by the president of the IOC, Henri de Baillet-Latour, that only IOC-designated people could perform such duties. If Hitler snubbed anyone it was on the first day when the black American Cornelius Johnson won the high jump and David Albritton was second. Owens was in fact snubbed by a different world leader. Although he received a ticker-tape welcome in New York and Cleveland, the president, Franklin D. Roosevelt, did not invite him to the White House, nor did he send him a congratulatory letter. Nonetheless, Hitler made it quite clear he that he thought the Americans should be ashamed of themselves for letting 'Negroes' win their medals for them and that he would never be seen shaking hands with any of them.

Charles spoke little about these games; he obviously missed the warmth and glamour of *la vie en rose* in Los Angeles. The one story he did tell was how, given hindsight (and the necessary weapon) he could have stopped Hitler and World War II before it started. While walking about alone in the old stadium at the Avus Race Track he found himself looking through wooden floorboards directly above Hitler in his open car. Other British athletes also felt that they had missed their chance to do the same thing when Hitler was just a few yards from them as he walked past the teams on his way into the stadium.

When Charles' brother, Walter, retired from racing, he acted as manager for Charles on certain occasions.

CHAPTER 6
The best all-rounder

Would Charles ever win the Best All-Rounder title? Was 1936 to be his year? On his return from the Olympics he certainly needed some good times over the relevant distances in order to be in the running. Unfortunately, he did not make a good start and in one of his first events the Coventry Godiva '50', he was beaten by S. W. Miles, the Best All-Rounder from 1935. Some consolation was gained by the fact that with Alf and Jack, the brothers won the team race.

Shortly after, in the classic Midland race, the Leamington '100', Charles returned to form. He had hoped to finish in a time of 4 hr. 25 min. but only managed 4 hr. 26 min. 48 sec. However, he was awarded a gold watch by the *The Bicycle* newspaper for breaking the 100-mile competition record. The MC&AC were also pleased as they won the team event, this time Charles was accompanied by H. Robinson and D. Jacobs.

Another page in cycling history was recorded when Charles put up the ride of his career to win the Manchester Wheelers' 12-hour race, with a ride that broke the British record. His ride was the second in two weeks to earn him a gold watch. Charles covered

"Cycling's"
"Best All-rounder"

Medallion
(Three-quarter Size)

The "BEST ALL-ROUNDERS" of 1936.

Their Performances and Awards.

1—C. HOLLAND, M.C. & A.C.
Rugby "50"
Leamington "100" 2.8.45
Manchester Wh. "12" 4.26.48
.. 246
Average Speed .. .. 22.097 m.p.h.
Awards: "Best All-Rounder" Trophy, Gold Medallion and First Certificate of Merit.

2—H. JAMES, Vegetarian.
Sharrow "50"
Bath Road "100" 2.8.5
Yorkshire C.F. "12" .. 4.29.20
Average Speed .. 244½
Awards: Silver Medallion with Gold Centre, Second Certificate of Merit and Bronze Team Medallion. .. 22.021 m.p.h.

3—A. N. HOLLAND, M.C. & A.C.
Belle Vue "50"
Westerley R.C. "100" .. 2.8.11
Manchester Wh. "12" .. 4.30.58
Average Speed .. 241½
Award: Silver Medallion and Third Certificate of Merit. .. 21.887 m.p.h.

4—R. W. HUDSON, Hull Thursday.
"Andy Wilson" "50" .. 2.7.20
Tees-side "100" .. 4.32.8
Yorkshire C.F. "12" .. 240½
Average Speed .. 21.876 m.p.h.
Awards: Bronze Medallion and Fourth Certificate of Merit.

5—H. EARNSHAW, Monckton.
Sheffield Central "50" .. 2.7.49
Bath Road "100" .. 4.33.50
Yorkshire Vegetarian "12" 241¾
Average Speed .. 21.839 m.p.h.
Awards: Fifth Certificate of Merit and Silver Team Medallion.

6—F. A. LIPSCOMBE, Century.
Velma "50" .. 2.7.31
Bath Road "100" .. 4.27.16
Anerley "12" .. 234
Average Speed .. 21.825 m.p.h.
Award: Sixth Certificate of Merit.

7—C. HEPPLESTON, Yorkshire R.C.
Godiva "50" .. 2.11.22
Yorkshire R.C. "100" .. 4.38.34
Yorkshire C.F. "12" .. 251½
Average Speed .. 21.782 m.p.h.
Award: Seventh Certificate of Merit.

8—N. HEY, Bronte Wh.
Rugby "50" .. 2.9.9
Yorkshire R.C. "100" .. 4.35.49
Yorkshire Vegetarian "12" 242½
Average Speed .. 21.730 m.p.h.
Award: Eighth Certificate of Merit.

9—S. M. BUTLER, Norwood Paragon.
Belle Vue "50" .. 2.10.6
Leamington "100" .. 4.35.4
Manchester Wh. "12" .. 241½
Average Speed .. 21.666 m.p.h.
Award: Ninth Certificate of Merit.

10—M. CLARK, Barnsley R.C.
"Andy Wilson" "50" .. 2.10.2
Gomersal "100" .. 4.34.30
E. Mids. R.A.A. "12" .. 238
Average Speed .. 21.587 m.p.h
Award: Tenth Certificate of Merit.

11—A. W. MARTIN, Monckton.
Rotherham "50" .. 2.8.12
Bath Road "100" .. 4.33.18
Yorkshire C.F. "12" .. 229½
Average Speed .. 21.500 m.p.h.
Awards: Eleventh Certificate of Merit and Silver Team Medallion.

12—H. H. PICKERSGILL, Vegetarian.
Belle Vue "50" .. 2.10.9
Tees-side "100" .. 4.38.6
Yorkshire Vegetarian "12" 237½
Average Speed .. 21.483 m.p.h.
Awards: Twelfth Certificate of Merit and Bronze Team Medallion.

A. HOLLENDER, Monckton.
Rotherham "50"
Bath Road "100" .. 2.8.53
Anfield "12" .. 4.41.43
Average Speed .. 233¼
Award: Silver Team Medallion. .. 21.355 m.p.h.

F. W. HILL, Vegetarian.
North London "50"
Westerley R.C. "100" .. 2.12.8
Yorkshire Vegetarian "12" 4.35.5
Average Speed .. 222½
Award: Bronze Team Medallion. .. 21.030 m.p.h.

TEAM SHIELD—Monckton C.C. (EARNSHAW, MARTIN and HOLLENDER)
Average Team Speed .. 21.565 m.p.h.
Award: "Best All-rounder" Team Shield to be held for one year.
SECOND "ALL-ROUNDER" TEAM—Vegetarian C. & A.C. (JAMES, PICKERSGILL and HILL)
Average Team Speed .. .. 21.511 m.p.h.

246 miles, S. M. Butler 241¾ miles and Alf Holland 241½ miles. This result meant that Charles leapt to the top of the BAR competition table, having done his three rides in three successive weekends. Alf also went above the previous leader, H. James, who retired from this race – so it was Holland first and Holland second.

By 23 September, James was back at the top of the table and Charles desperately needed to do 2 hr. 10 min. in a '50' to regain his position. The Rugby '50', the last qualifying race of the season, was where the battle would be fought. James actually won the race in 2 hr. 8 min. 29 sec. but Charles' time of 2 hr. 8 min. 45 sec. was good enough for him to overtake James and return to the top of the table. When James heard this he sportingly declared, 'well we had a ride for it anyway'.

Charles had at last achieved his ambition of winning the coveted title of Best All-Rounder. W. J. Mills, the editor of *The Bicycle*, paid him a great tribute when he described him as:

The Best All-Rounder, not in its narrow sense of best average in certain particular road events, but in its real sense of best at all types of cycling. Holland's record for the year includes successes at almost every possible type of racing: time trials, massed starts, track racing, in fact the full programme in which every clubman likes to indulge. The specialist 'pot hunter' may confine himself to his little round of events at distances that he finds brings in the rewards, but the real clubman runs through the gamut of events, taking pleasure, if not prizes, in all and sundry. Of such a type is the dusky Midlander, taking all the sport can offer in his stride.

Charles' average speed over 50 miles, 100 miles and 12 hours was 22.097 mph, and it was the first time in the competition that the average speed exceeded 22 mph. H. James, who was a very close second, did 22.021 mph and Charles' brother, Alf, who came third, did 21.887 mph. As Charles had previously been third, and second twice, it was the general feeling that it was 'right and proper' for him to win particularly as the opposition was stronger than ever.

'What sort of man is Charles Holland?' asked *Cycling*:

He is four inches short of 6 feet; is single, weighs 11½ stone, smokes and drinks occasionally. Has black sleek hair parted on the side, and a most infectious smile. Consequently, he is a great favourite with the girls. Actually he prefers the massed-start type of racing to English time trials – but is a good mixer and a real clubman. Like all champions he is modest. His greatest ambition is to win the world's road championship.

On Sunday 25 October Charles attempted to crown his list of 1936 records by making a bid for no less than four Road Record Association (RRA) records in one ride, namely: the Edinburgh to York, the 12-hour, the Edinburgh to London, and the 24-hour. Starting in darkness, with icy cold rain, it was hoped that the weather would improve during the course of the ride. However, strong winds put paid to a record-breaking ride and it was discontinued at Chester-le-Street.

In January 1937 the annual Best-All-Rounder event took place at the Royal Albert Hall but for Charles there was one big difference, he was the winner. On this occasion he was invited to sign the *Golden Book of Cycling*, a book described as being specially made of vellum leaves, bound in vellum and gold and constructed by craftsmen to last throughout many centuries. The dedication above the signatures begins: 'In the pages of this book dedicated to future generations of cyclists are inscribed descriptions of great

Finally, Charles wins the BAR competition and is presented with the trophy by Roland E. Dangerfield at the annual prize-giving event in January 1937.

deeds done in the cycling world, and against each record appears the signature of the performer.'

Amongst the other recognition he received was a telegram of congratulations from the Lord Mayor of Birmingham, and a celebratory dinner, organised by four local clubs, was held in his honour in Walsall. A five-course meal, followed by speeches, toasts, entertainment – provided by singers and comedians – and the presentation of an illuminated address (a highly decorative gilded certificate), were the order of the day. Aldridge, not to be outdone, also presented Charles with a magnificent illuminated address, which as well as listing his cycling achievements reads,

'Throughout his career he has shown himself to be a good sports-man, a cheerful loser, a modest winner, and this address is to testify to the honour and pride in which he is held by the inhabitants of Aldridge.'

In addition to attending functions Charles also found time to write two lengthy articles for *Cycling*. The first on massed-start racing was in reply to a feature in the same magazine headlined 'Let's be British' in which the author (K.M.D.) had said, 'that the movement to substitute massed-start racing for the present time trial system of racing was ill-advised and injurious to cycle sport as a whole.' Charles disagreed and this was his reply:

❝I have dabbled in most branches of the cycling game, time trials, massed-start racing and on the track and I'm not prepared to say which is the best or that I personally enjoy one in preference to the other. The brightest feature of the game is the tremendous growth, and massed-start racing has done its share in making cycling popular among the general public.

Reviewing the sporting side of the road game, there are many flaws, even in time-trial system. The best man does not always win. It often happens that the difference in the weather conditions between the time of the start of the first man and the last man off means an advantage of several seconds and sometimes minutes to one of them, which of course, does not occur in the massed start ...

The suggestion that Opperman was once overtaken, after making a breakaway in a stage of the Tour de France, by a rider being towed by an official's car, even it it is true, is only on a par with what is alleged happened to Southall in an unpaced time trial on the Continent when he was overtaken in the same manner, which proves nothing regarding the merits of the time trial against the massed start. Personally, on my visits abroad I have always found the game played just as we in

England endeavour to play it, which is may the best man win.

The greatest honour a cyclist can gain is to win a world or Olympic championship, and as these are run on massed-start lines we should do everything to encourage our riders to gain the coveted honours. By organising more massed-start races our riders will gain the necessary experience to compete on favourable terms with the Continentals.

The occasion of the French team's visit to Donington, when they gave us such a licking – no we shall not forget it – was an example of English inexperience, but I am certain they could not do it again …

Englishmen have taught the world how to play most games, but countries who have specialised in a particular game can now give us lessons. Some of us have already taken advantage of things we have learned abroad and the times in unpaced trials have improved accordingly … And so I finish, looking forward to another season of massed-start thrills, track racing excitement, and that indescribable something which will always maintain the popularity of the time trial. ""

The second, less controversial article, was on, 'The Control of Road Sport', and he began emphatically:

" Yes, I am in favour of control. Our sport is alone among national pastimes in not having a centralised body, with the authority to direct and manage its affairs and, therefore, lacks the stability and dignity attached to other sports … While red tape and unnecessary regulations should be avoided, to direct and regulate the sport properly, strict rules as to the conduct and promotion of events, the equipment and behaviour of riders, and the powers and duties of local councils and committees must be clearly laid down. ""

The Six-Day Event to be held at Wembley was the first major event for Charles of the 1937 racing season. Major in more ways than one, it necessitated his change from amateur to professional status. Along with W. F. Burl, he joined the cash ranks. In a packed stadium the event was started by Gracie Fields, the competitors were described as whirling dervishes speeding away without rhyme or reason. For Charles, it was a short though probably not sweet experience. This is his story of the course of events.

❝❝I turn professional

On April 21st 1937, I called at the offices of the National Cyclists' Union, and received from Mr H. N. Crowe, the secretary, my first international licence as a professional. It was just ten years ago that

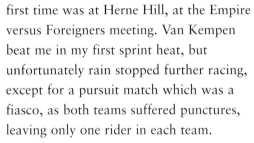

I competed in my first cycle race, never dreaming then that I should be so fascinated by the 'bike game' that I should eventually make my living at it.

I learned a lot as an amateur. When I was beaten I asked myself why. I recalled everything I had done prior to and during the race, and tried to find my faults. Cycle racing is all ups and downs and in ten years I had plenty of both. When luck has been against me I have consoled myself with the thought that next time perhaps it would be in my favour.

That is the position I feel I am in at the moment. I have competed twice as a professional, and so far I have not had too much luck. The first time was at Herne Hill, at the Empire versus Foreigners meeting. Van Kempen beat me in my first sprint heat, but unfortunately rain stopped further racing, except for a pursuit match which was a fiasco, as both teams suffered punctures, leaving only one rider in each team.

Of course the big event I had in mind then was the Six-day Race. While I had learnt a lot about cycle racing in the past ten years; believe me, I felt almost the same as when I competed in my first novice race as midnight approached on May 16th last. I had trained really hard for this event, and the finishing work I had done in Belgium on the small track at Liège had put a little

The British and Australian riders, who were training in Wandre near Liège, Belgium for the Wembley Six-Day race, take a break.

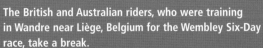

more speed in my legs, and I was looking forward to putting up a good performance as I felt as fit as I had ever done. In the first few hours I had three falls due to the lack of understanding between my partner, Roger Deneef, and myself in the changeovers.

Roger hurt his ankle badly in one spill and I seemed to have bruises on every part of my body, but professional riders, I learned were really tough, and with the hectic jams, terrific sprints, and the deafening applause from the crowd I forgot my minor troubles and concentrated on pushing or swinging my partner to get the maximum benefit from the speed without further crashes.

Towards the end of the first session we were mastering the art of changing and pulled back one or two laps that we had previously lost.

Training at Wandre, Belgium, from left to right, front row: Opperman (Australia), Ridgers (Australia), Southall, Holland, Buckley (Australia), Smith (Australia), Burl, back row: Grant, Cozens, Charlier (Belgium) and another rider.

We had both won a few sprints and things were not too bad, but everyone seemed glad when the neutral period came and we could get snatches of rest. I could not sleep a wink on the hard beds and my abrasions seemed much worse than they really were, but I am told that very few riders sleep the first day.

However the Six-day Race has passed into history now, and I will finish this part of my story by telling you of the smash that has kept me off the bicycle for four weeks so that my training has been delayed.

During the second night the jam is on; two teams gain a lap; we are in the chase; I take over from Roger and I can see the tail of the field just in front. Putting in all I know I make a lap. I should have been content to stop in this position, but seeing an opening I made for it with the idea of getting well placed before handing over to my partner, but my luck was out. Two riders making a change, swerved and the three of us piled up. I got up a little shaken and it was not until I reached my bunk that I realised what had happened. My collarbone was broken and I was out of the race.

The following days were very painful in more ways than one but after a fortnight I began to get about a little on the machine and was looking forward to riding in the Crystal Palace race. But that was not to be. One evening, during a stroll, in some long grass I tripped in a rabbit hole, fell and, of course landed on the injured shoulder. An X-ray examination revealed that I had fractured the bone again. However, I am very pleased to say that my shoulder is going on fine and I am training hard, for my greatest ambition has been realised and I have been accepted for the Tour de France.

I do not think I can get absolutely racing fit for the start next Wednesday, but as the tour takes nearly a month to complete I hope to ride myself into my best form in the first few days. With reasonable luck I feel confident that I can ride through this great race. However next week I will tell you more about that.

Charles had some continental race experience but had no idea of what lay ahead in Tour.

CHAPTER 7
Dispatches from the Tour

❝ I am hoping to be among them at the finish

On the eve of my departure for Paris [Saturday 26 June] I look back on the past two weeks almost as though they were a dream.

I had signed a contract to ride in the Tour de France and at the same time posted to a few friends, including the Editor of *Cycling*, intimation that I had done so. Exactly two weeks before the race was due to start I met *Cycling's* Editor at his Birmingham office. He had two newspapers with him, the French *L'Auto* and an English daily. Much to my amazement, *L'Auto*, which newspaper is, of course, the promoter of the Tour, stated that neither Bill Burl nor myself would be riding in the race. The English newspaper gave similar information, and as the writer was supposed to know something about it, I was in an awkward predicament in view of the arrangements I had already made.

The actual 'gram

Immediately we decided to send a telegram to *L'Auto* asking for a statement on the position, and it was not until the next day that I received a final telegram – sent care of *Cycling's* Birmingham office, which ran as follows: 'Following your wire dated yesterday agree engagement if you agree yours – *L'Auto*.' Naturally, I agreed to the new arrangement, whereby Bill Burl, Pierre Gachon of Canada and myself would comprise the British Empire's Ace team. Previously, it was decided that we should ride as individuals.

I cannot tell you anything about Gachon, as I have not had the pleasure of meeting him so far; yet Bill Burl's performance in the Crystal Palace race a fortnight ago must have given him plenty of confidence, although I was sorry indeed to learn of his crash in Ostend. Bill then cracked two ribs, and in consequence he has been

The British Empire Ace team, from left to right, Bill Burl, Charles Holland and Pierre Gachon, complete with their *L'Auto* yellow and black bicycles and the two tyres they were allowed to carry .

unable to train at all during the past week. He has been in great pain, but he intends to be fit for the start of the race on Wednesday. It is a terrible misfortune that he should have had this accident – Bill has said since that had he realised the Tour de France was so near he would never have risked himself in the Ostend race. However, all these things are in the luck of the game.

Owing to my collarbone trouble, I too, have been unable to get in all the training I needed, although during the past eight days I have been averaging 100 miles a day. The first two days were on a tandem. My partner was of similar build so we were able to take turns in the front and, in consequence, I was able to give my injured shoulder some rest. The bone has set firmly, but the arm seems quite weak and is easily tired. On the Monday of last week, I managed 80 miles quite comfortably, averaging about 18 miles an hour, and decided to have a longer ride the next day.

With the intention of having a nonstop ride I fixed two bottles on the handlebars, and I slung one of the continental linen bags (*musettes*) filled with sandwiches and fruit across my shoulders. My good intentions were soon baulked by a downpour of rain, which necessitated my caping up, for I was not anxious to get wet through and at the same time spoil my lunch. So I had to carry on much slower for about an hour. I rode about 120 miles that day, the last 60 of which I did at 'evens' and, as I was riding heavy steel wheels complete with mudguards and only a 65-inch gear, I felt quite pleased with myself.

The following day I was content to do about 100 miles, but I made the pace slightly faster, the last 50 being covered inside 2 hr. 22 min. Having done no fast pedalling since the London Six-day Race, I was still using a 65-inch gear. and consequently my legs were a little stiff, so on the Thursday I took things much easier. doing a steady 60 miles and having a good massage in the morning.

I was looking forward to a busman's holiday in the afternoon, listening to the Isle of Man race. I have listened to horse racing, tennis, cricket, and the motorcycle races in the Isle of Man, and have enjoyed them, but the cycle race description was far from good.

However, to get back to my story, I rode another 130 miles on Friday, averaging about 16 mph, not stopping for food or drink, but having what I carried. During the whole of my career I have never trained over such long distances without stopping for food but I can say that I am feeling better for it. As an amateur I had plenty of races in which to find my staying powers, but so far this year I have had no racing that calls for stamina.

More preparation

Today (I am writing this on Saturday evening) I rode just over 100 miles. Tomorrow I shall be travelling most of the day, which leaves only two more days to finish off my training. But there will be plenty of riding to look forward to after that. I am hoping that the first two stages are not too fast. If I had been able to get in plenty of racing this year, I should not mind how the stages went. Still, if I do not have any unforeseen trouble such as crashes, punctures and so on, I am hoping to be amongst them at the finish. I know it is going to be mighty tough, particularly when we hit the mountains. I understand that the experts cannot agree which is the harder, the going up or coming down. The riders who live near the mountains practise, so I am told, coming round the bends at terrific speeds – and when the gradients are about four times as long as those in the Isle of Man, cornering at high speed plays an important part. I hope to learn all about it!

Looking down the list of entries I notice a few names of riders I have met at different times. Charpentier, the Olympic Games road champion, and Goujon, who finished just behind me in that race, are old rivals of mine, as we have raced against one another on several occasions. I have been trying to pick out the riders who will be nursed along by their teams. Maes, winner of last year's Tour, Vervaecke and Danneels will be Belgium's 'probables', but it is harder still to pick out the Frenchmen, as Chocque, Lapébie, Le Grèves and Speicher are only half of the famous French Aces. Bartali, by virtue of his win in the Tour of Italy, will probably star amongst the Italians.

The cyclists travelled from London, Victoria on the Golden Arrow, with very little luggage and strangely enough no bikes. At their departure it was reported: 'Holland was looking particularly fit and said that he was only 50 miles short of his training plan ... His collarbone has now set sufficiently to allow arm and shoulder movement's necessary for cycling. Burl was in good trim, too, although the ribs he damaged in Ostend still pain him.'

Although I think the ultimate winner will be found among these riders, the chances of many others are almost as good. The deciding factor will be the teamwork and, as France and Belgium have the biggest teams, it is almost a foregone conclusion that the winner will be found among either of these.

Tour fever

Burl and I reached Paris at 6 p.m. on Sunday, 27 June, the day before we were due to report at the offices of *L'Auto*. It is impossible almost for me to set down my thoughts as I stepped out of the station into the streets of the 'Gay City'.

So much had happened in the weeks previous that I had not had time to think about the tremendous undertaking I had set myself when I accepted the invitation to ride in the Tour de France. When we arrived in Paris, however, there came over me a feeling of panic and I realised the imminence of what would probably be the greatest cycle racing adventure that had fallen the lot of any Englishman for very many years. I was anxious to be doing something; to be getting ready for the great day, but Paris is more than ever *en fête* on Sunday evenings, and we were unable to do anything that night. We rose early next morning, Monday, and immediately paid our respects to the officials at *L'Auto* offices.

At once we were supplied with a machine each, spare tyres, goggles, waterproof riding jacket and a suitcase to hold our spare clothing during the Tour. The idea of the latter is that everyone shall have similar equipment, thus discouraging riders from carrying more than necessary. Some of the riders left to their own choice in the matter would send large trunks on the lorries that take our baggage ahead from stage to stage.

It is usual for the rider in the Tour de France to fit his own saddle and handlebars, and we spent the best part of that day fitting these items to our machines, adjusting the gears. brakes, etc. All the bicycles are painted yellow with black lines [*L'Auto* was printed in black on yellow paper], and on the head tube the name *L'Auto* is transferred, whilst the name of the rider is painted on the top tube. No advertising of any description is allowed in connection with the bicycles we ride.

Burl and I managed to get about 20 miles riding in before it became too dark, and although the machines are very different in frame design from our own we believed that we should get used to riding them.

'Tour fever' was rampant in Paris during those two days before the race started. Everywhere we went cameras clicked at us, and every newspaper published was full of Tour de France pictures. We both developed cramp from signing autographs!

Charles's Tour contract

The actual contract between M. H. Desgrange, Editor of *L'Auto,* and Charles, '*coureur, cycliste professionnel majeur*', shows the nature of the 1937 Tour and illustrates how different a world it was to what it is today.

In the contract Desgrange agrees to provide the riders with the '*accessoires necessaries*' listed as spokes, spanners, adhesive tape, goggles (maximum 6 pairs) jerseys, mussettes (small cotton shoulder bags for food) etc., with the exception of shorts, leggings and caps. The contract also states that none of these articles are to be thrown on the road even '*au moment de l'effort final*'. In the midst of all this the riders are also asked to send their chest and height measurements.

The hotel rooms would have two beds and a drink would be provided for the riders on their arrival. Baths would be available at a 'bath house' or at the hotel. Their meals, breakfast (*petit dejeuner or dejeuner du matin*), lunch and dinner were to be chosen by the Directeur sportif and changes could only be made to meals which did not incur a price supplement. Charles would have enjoyed reading in his contract that a daily ration of beer (two bottles), milk, mineral water and one bottle of wine, were also included.

The contract states that at the end of each stage medical care, massages and the inspection, repair and cleaning of their bikes would be provided. It is spelt out that the medical care was for sores, wounds, stomach aches etc. and that any 'fortifiants, reconstituants and *drogues* (drugs)' should be kept by the cyclist.

Entrants are also informed that they must take their pump and their spare tyres to their room and that any loss would result in a bill being sent to the rider.

Tuesday – the day before the start

Of course we suddenly remembered many items that we might require during the race, and we went on a shopping expedition. [It seems they bought caps, vests, leg warmers, shorts, socks etc.] That day, too, our bicycles had to be sealed and we had to sign various forms of agreement. For the rest of the day we took things fairly easily. Pierre Gachon, our team-mate, was introduced to us. We learned that Gachon was a Frenchman by birth, but he had emigrated to Canada and was entered in the Tour as an individual to represent the country of his adoption. When our last minute entries were accepted, as you now know, we were formed into a team of three in the name of the British Empire. During that evening we discussed a plan of campaign and then went to bed early, for we had to be up at 5 a.m. in the morning.

The team of three planned to stay together for the first three stages and, in the event of a puncture, the other two would wait so that regaining lost time would be easier. Only when they were 20 km from the finish would each race for himself.

I said we went to bed, but speaking for myself it was not to sleep. My mind was full of what might happen on the morrow, and the waking dreams that I experienced were worse even than what was to follow in reality.

Breakfast a la Tour!

We were up at 4 a.m. and at 5 a.m., after a massage, we sat down to a meal of soup, eggs on beefsteak and fruit. This was certainly a new line for me, but as everyone else seemed to be enjoying this strange breakfast, I did full justice to it myself.

We were all ready in racing kit and proceeded to *L'Auto*'s offices for the official checkup and to sign the register, which is done at

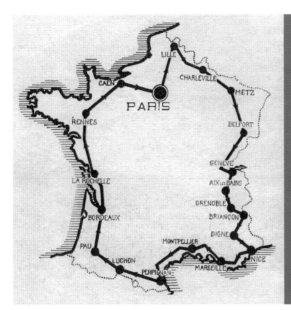

The 1937 race, which took place between 3 June to 25 July, was the 31st Tour, covering 4,415 km (2,759 miles in 20 stages, with 98 riders from nine countries (Belgium, Italy, Spain, Holland, Luxembourg, Switzerland, Britain, Germany, France) taking part. The race was started by Antonin Magne, winner of the Tour in 1931, 1932 and second to Sylvère Maes in 1936.

the beginning and end of every stage. The race proper started at 9.30 a.m. but for nearly an hour and a half we rode in mass formation around Paris to let the thousands of people, who were closely packed on each side of the streets, have a look at the Tour riders. The screaming headlines in the press, and the almost continuous broadcasts on the radio, are exceeded in enthusiasm only by the hysteria of the French people themselves.

The feeding station

At Amiens, the halfway point, there was a Control and here we were handed a satchel containing two bidons. You may imagine that those first served made a dash for it and the field was once more very split up. The group was only formed again after a long chase by those behind. only to be split up once more when we struck the stretch of *pavé* (cobblestones).

Some of the Belgium team befriended Charles and sent him photographs, including this one.

Most of the riders seemed very tired at about 20 miles to go and the *pavé* was so bad that it was hopeless trying to hang on to a wheel. Riders passed and were re-passed as their energies revived and sagged. There were numerous spills along this cruel road.

It was here that I began to have difficulty in steering my machine. It was very stiff and bounced all over the road. I dropped back further, but kept on, knowing that the end was near, and it was with a sigh of relief that I reached the horse-racing track at Lille to ride a final lap. I finished 52nd, 15 minutes behind the leader. When I examined my machine it was a wonder I had finished at all, as the head tube had two long splits in it; a few more miles and the forks would have left the frame.

There was a terrific crowd at Lille, all along the streets, and the stands and the enclosures at the track were packed. It was quite a task getting to the Control to sign off and then to the hotel for a bath and dinner. [It is not known what happened to Gachon apart from the fact that he never arrived at Lille and was eliminated on the first day as a defaulter.]

The second day

The second stage of the Tour, from Lille to Charleville, was not quite so far but, as we encountered much more *pavé*, it was just as hard as the long journey. We left Lille at 11 a.m. and it was raining a little. The wet *pavé* was the cause of many crashes, especially where there were tramlines as well. In the country, gravel or dirt paths bordered the road and it was much easier to ride on them, although there were more crashes caused through getting on and off the paths. On one occasion I was making for a narrow and fairly smooth strip about 12 inches wide, when a Frenchman came from the left and a Belgian from the right, and they hit me simultaneously. I got the path, however, the Belgian hitting the *pavé* and the Frenchman the grass!

Going through the town of Maubeuge, just before the halfway point, I was riding with a leading group of about 20 riders. Negotiating some tramlines going downhill a rider crashed, and swerving to avoid him I crashed too. I fell on my left side, and although somewhat bruised I am pleased to say that the collarbone stood up to the fall. I had a long solo chase until Paul Chocque came along, he had crashed too, and doing 'bit-and-bit' we eventually caught the field. In the meantime two riders had broken away, Archambaud and another. I made several attempts to break away, having been told that we had only 15 kilometres to do. I found, however, that the 15 kilometres were nearer 30, and I was caught by several small groups as I began to tire.

We finished on the cycle track at Charleville, but we did not ride around it as it was too wet. It had poured down most of the way and the riders were in a terrible state. My efforts over the last few miles had put me in a fairly good position and I finished close behind the leaders. On general classification after two days' racing I found myself 38th in the list.

Metz, Friday

Charles finished the second stage in 5 hr. 20 min. 2 sec. in a group of forty riders classed as sixth. The winner in 5 hr. 18 min. 31 sec. was Majerus of Luxembourg. On this the second day Burl had a burst tyre when rounding a corner at speed and this brought him down heavily. In addition to hurting his ribs again, his gears were damaged and he could only use a low one. He continued bravely but arrived at the Control after it was closed and was eliminated.

The third stage of the Tour, Charleville to Metz, was about 100 miles. The roads were quite good, as there was no dreaded *pavé*. There were quite a few stiff climbs compared with any English courses I know, but the rush down the other side of these hills for a mile or so was a thrilling experience. The road took a winding course through well-wooded country. It would have delighted the tourist intent only on easy riding. The *peloton* was split up several times, but there were no serious breakaways up to 30 miles from the finish.

I do not know what happened after that as I had the misfortune to puncture. I lost about five minutes, as I am not yet familiar with all the details of the new machine. I had enjoyed a rather easy ride up to then so I went flat out until I came to a stiff and long climb, at which I only just staggered to the top, but urged on by the huge crowds I caught a Frenchman, a Swiss, a Spaniard and a German. They made me do most of the work in front and, as I was anxious to arrive at the finish before the Control closed, it was a case of having to go if I intended to keep in the Tour.

And a sprint to finish!

I was really annoyed, however, for so soon as the finish was in sight they all tried to sprint me. The crowd was so packed that only two could really ride side by side, but I felt so mad that they had taken me for the mug all this time that I slammed in the top gear, pushed all I knew, and squeezed through the crowd to win this minor sprint by a length. I finished 81st, 12 minutes behind the leader, and ten other riders were behind me.

Charles, now a team of one, finished this stage in 4 hr. 25 min. 43 sec. and was actually classed as 61st. Generatti of Italy was the winner of this 100-mile stage in 4 hr. 13 min. 2 sec..

I am still in the Tour!

My experience in the French Alps

Today, Monday 5 July, is the first rest day of the Tour, and everyone is very pleased to have this pause.

The halt is at Geneva in Switzerland. I wonder how many English folk have realised that part of the course passes through another country. I certainly did not know this interesting fact. If you look at the map, however, you will see that a tip of Switzerland to the southwest of Lake Geneva juts into French territory and the Tour short-cuts across this 'peninsular' into the French Alps to the west and south.

The last two days have been really gruelling for, in addition to the mountains we have had to climb, the weather has been exceedingly hot. The countryside is looking really marvellous now; we have a chance to look round sometimes! I understand, however, that up to the present we have been experiencing the calm before the storm.

On Saturday, riding from Metz to Belfort, as we were touring along enjoying the ride I was talking to Paul Chocque. He was telling me of the mountains we had in front of us. Paul is one of the very few riders who can speak English. It was at this point that

I collected another puncture. I changed tyres as quickly as I could and gave chase, but I had lost five minutes. I caught several individuals, but as they would not work in front I jumped away alone in an effort to catch the *peloton*. I had seen riders being paced occasionally by cars, so when one slowed down in front of me and the driver made signs for me to tuck in behind, I did so. An official car had been observing me so I thought that everything was in order. It is impossible to ride unpaced when chasing the leading group, as there are streams of following cars. However, for taking this shelter for about two miles I was put last in the order of arrival at Belfort, 23 minutes later than my actual arrival time. I consider that I was penalised to show how strictly the rules are observed, and to vindicate the officials in view of statements that have been made from time to time alleging that they have a convenient 'blind eye'. [Charles was also fined 100 francs.]

On the fourth stage of the race from Metz to Belfort the climb up the Ballon d'Alsace of 4,000 ft. seemed as though it would never end. Up and up, twisting and turning, and to make matters worse there were scores of motor vehicles blasting forth fumes that choked us, and sometimes stalling in front of us so that we were actually brought to a standstill. The heat had melted the road surfaces and when we arrived at Belfort we were filthier than after the rainy second stage between Lille and Charleville. I had tar all over my legs, arms and face, and I needed a fresh rig out for the following day's race.

Sunday is the holiday of the week on the Continent, and there were hundreds of thousands of spectators all along the route from Belfort to Geneva, a total of 189 miles. We left Belfort at 5.30 a.m. to complete the three sections of this stage to Geneva. The first section was a massed-start race to Lons-le-Saunier (110 miles). I finished with the *peloton*, was classed 13th, and received the general time of 5 hr. 38 min. 1 sec., compared with the winner's (Puppo) 5 hr. 36 min. 15 sec.. The second stage to Champagnole (21 miles) was a time trial by teams. I was put with the Italians, but the road was up and down and those boys simply sprinted up the hills and flew down the other sides. It was a scorching hot day and, whether it was the heat or the strange array of foodstuffs we had for lunch at Lons-le-Saunier, I do not know, but my legs became weaker and weaker and I had to drop out of the team and ride alone.

I felt terrible

The distance was only 21 miles, but we had another 58 miles to do in the third section before the day's riding was completed. This last race was again in line and from the word 'go' it was one mad rush. I felt terrible at first, but I observed most of the others were having a bad time too. We seemed to be climbing all the time, gradual slopes at first, but getting steeper and steeper. Now the riders who had been forcing the pace were dropping back, but I kept slogging alone and, except for a few who had got away earlier on, I found myself making the pace. A few miles further in I was away with a small group of eight or nine, including Maes, Archambaud, Bartali and Martano. I do not know how high we actually climbed but this ride seemed even worse than the Ballon d' Alsace. It was with a sigh of relief that we reached the top. And now came the rush down the other side. It was nerve-racking. After making such a great effort to be at the front with a good lead on the *peloton*, I intended to stay there, if possible. Archambaud and Martano, however, got away. Speaking to Sylvère Maes later he agreed that the Italian Martano was absolutely mad in the way he took that suicidal downhill, and Maes can certainly go downhill himself. Most of the hairpin bends were just loose gravel and, as we swept down at 50 miles an hour, it seems to me a marvel that we reached the bottom on wheels. Yet what about the two who had gained over a minute on us – phew!

We finally reached the city of Geneva, after several attempts had been made by Maes and Archambaud to break away. The finish was on a wide main road all closed in with stands packed with spectators, and in the sprint between our group I managed to screw the others down. I was finally placed 27th in the stage and 64th in the general classification.

PS These first five days of racing have made a wonderful difference to me and I am now feeling quite good.

Leaving Geneva

We had a fine send off on Tuesday, [6 July] leaving at 11 a.m. with Aix-les-Bains as our objective, a distance of 113 miles.

The sun was already very hot, and before long we were bathed in perspiration. There were two mountain passes to cross. I kept my position as nearly as possible in the middle. So far, I have not dared really to extend myself, as it is essential that I have a good reserve in case of punctures and other troubles. Still I am doing much better than I expected and I was in a very good position descending the second slope when suddenly my gear went wrong. Only the 58 inch would engage and on the flat I had to pedal furiously. I stopped and adjusted it so that I could use the 71 inch and then I had the misfortune to puncture the rear tyre. Tar seemed to be on everything and changing was a messy job. I knew it was hopeless trying to get up with the leaders again, so I fiddled with the gears and finally fixed them correctly. I could see a posse of eighteen riders coming along in the distance, so I joined them. Included in this group were Lapébie and Le Grèves, the French aces, and I enjoyed the run of about 40 miles, taking it in turns at the front. The scenery was magnificent.

A bunch of riders all coming in together are all given the same time, but the winner of the sprints listed in front of the others. It looks better to be 28th than 46th! Although Le Grèves is reckoned to be the best road man sprinter in France I beat him and finished first in our group.

During the first three hours of riding in the Aix-les-Bains to Grenoble stage the following day, I thought it was a Tour de Luxe I was riding in, but everything

The leading bunch in the sixth stage from Geneva to Aix-les-Bains, Charles may be seen just above the pillion rider's head.

these professionals do is done with a purpose and their purpose this time was to prepare for the climb over Galibier, 8,000 feet up! After snatching a satchel of food and drink at the foot of the mountain, the big push started; up and up for about 4,000 feet, then a fall of about 2,000 feet. And now with gears of about 49 inches we were struggling up again, mile after mile. The roads were good at first, but they became much worse and, halfway to the top, cool air was noticeable. We had been glad when water was thrown over us earlier in the day, but now, in spite of our efforts, the cool winds were really chilling.

Looking up, I glimpsed the snow and it seemed impossible that there should be a way through those jagged rocks. In places our tyres sank into thick mud where the snow had melted.

Bartali, of Italy, is the marvel of hill climbers, he must have been minutes in front of me, but looking over the sides of the

This sixth stage included the first of the 'proper' mountains with the Col des Aravis at 4,800 ft. and the Col de Tamie at 3,000 ft. Over the second of these Charles, accompanied by Archambaud and Goujon, was only 4 min. 50 sec. behind the leader Vervaecke, of Belgium, who reached the top of both cols first. It was announced at the end of this stage that certain riders, including Speicher, of France, had been fined 25 francs for following too close behind motor vehicles. This may be compared with Charles fine of 100 francs plus his time penalty of 23 minutes!

road, I could see dozens of riders far down behind me, and I was looking down at the snow, which previously I had thought impossible to reach. The crowd got denser and the police whistle shrilled out as I reached the top. I say the top but we did not go over the actual summit but through a long tunnel. This was a nightmare after the bright daylight. It seemed like we groped our way through it for about half a mile. There were several tunnels afterwards but they were illuminated. There must have been a failure in the lighting system in the first one. The descent was awful – rough roads, stones bruising one's legs as they shot out from under the tyres and cars getting in the way. It started to rain and I was as cold as though I had been competing in an early morning race in England on a March day.

Then bang! Yes, I had thought it was impossible for a tyre to stand such treatment, I was riding on the front rim, dangerously wobbling all over the road, but I pulled up without mishap. My hands were so numb that I had difficulty in changing and riders were constantly passing me. When I was on my way again I really had the wind-up. What if the tyre was to roll off when I was at speed on one of those terrible hairpin bends? As the conditions

Bartali of Italy, renowned for hill climbing, tackles Galibier during the seventh stage. Note the unmade road and bleak terrain.

became warmer, I felt better and I joined a group of other riders.

The roads were quite good again and the corners not so severe, though we were now taking them at 40 and sometimes 50 mph. Then a thunderstorm let loose and I was forced to ease a little on the bends, as I could feel the tyre creeping. Danneels with two other Belgians, Le Grèves and another Frenchman, Mersch and two Germans were amongst a posse of about 20 riders, and I had to keep doing a series of sprints to overhaul them after easing on the bends. However, all's well that ends well, and I finished with the bunch. I was the 50th arrival on this stage and 57th in the general classification.

We were still in the Alps on Thursday, 8 July, riding from Grenoble to Briançon, 121 miles. It was up and down all the way,

Charles' brother, Walter, wrote to him on 7 July telling him, 'Lots of folk I know who in the ordinary way are not a bit interested in cycling have spoken to me about your effort. It has caught the fancy of a lot of people, the way you are struggling against the odds and there is no doubt your reputation is considerably enhanced. This is exactly what I told you when I advised you to ride. Incidentally, the French papers have made much of the fact you carry a watch, one cartoon showing you with an alarm clock, a cuckoo clock and an hourglass attached to your bike. Mother was very upset when you were fined 100 francs, she thought it was a 100 quid at least. I hope to get over to see you during the last two days so keep your pecker up.'

and the country was of a very wild nature. The villages were very antiquated and no decent sized motor vehicle would be able to get through some of the streets. The inhabitants seemed to be of a different world. A few uttered words of encouragement, but others sat silently in little groups and seemed to resent this intrusion into their peaceful life. Perhaps they were amazed at the spectacle of 70 riders dashing through their village, garbed in all the colours of the rainbow. Whatever the reason, the result was that we had fewer drinks handed to us than usual. I went for miles without a welcome bidon or bottle, and in consequence, I did not feel so good. I finished again with Danneels and Le Grèves, Mersch and about twelve others. There was no sprint at the finish as there was no room between the spectators, and we ambled in.

Gaining confidence in the mountains
Next morning, Friday, we set off at 8.30 a.m. for the Briançon–Digne stage, a distance of 138 miles. The field was now getting

smaller every day and at breakfast, Majerus and Clemens, who were eliminated yesterday, were getting autographed photos of all the riders. It seemed a pity that the former, a pleasant faced, lanky fellow who had been the first to wear the Yellow Jersey, had to abandon the Tour. No doubt, his early effort told on him.

We started to climb a rough road as soon as we were out of Briançon and I should think we went up 4,000 feet. It was a terrible climb, loose stones caused the wheels to slip, and the field was quickly spread out. I seemed to lose my confidence going down the first mountain that day. I thought that the roads were worse than ever. Although I had a good position at the summit, I was nearly last at the bottom. I felt good otherwise and started to make up for lost time, catching quite a number of riders up the second mountain. Now I was gaining more confidence.

Bartali, the leader, whilst swooping down the mountains, skidded, crashed into a parapet, went over the side and landed in a fast-flowing stream at the bottom of a ravine. Carrried by the current and nearly drowned, he was rescued by his team-mate, Camusso. He remounted and finished 33rd in the stage – ten minutes behind the leader – and retained his position at the head of the aggregate time list!

It was the same over the third col, but I was very grieved that after I had outridden certain riders, they passed me again, being pushed up the hill by relays of spectators, and finally, after I had passed them, they repassed me again being towed by a car.

The next was about the fastest descent I have yet made. I joined an Italian, a Spaniard and a Frenchman, all experts on the mountains, but I was intent on beating those who had laughed at me when they were being towed. Yes, I had my laugh when I pushed my wheel in front of theirs at the end of the final sprint. I was 36th in the stage and 52nd in the classification.

Today we are having a well-earned rest at Digne. There are 62 riders left in the Tour and Sylvère Maes, last year's winner, is now in the lead. He is a likeable fellow and we get on very well together. In fact, his team-mates are a happy-go-lucky crowd and work together better than any other combination. I passed four of them yesterday on the mountains, Danneels, Deltour, Kint and Meulenberg, but it was beautiful to watch the way they rode together when they caught me later on the flat. I did about 50 miles with them to the finish. I did my share at the front, but it was very noticeable how some others simply hung onto the back.

I am getting very fit now and hope to finish the Tour, but I realise anything can happen between here and Paris. I have seen too many aces come unstuck during the past two weeks, so I will just hope for the best.

Along the Mediterranean coast

We left Digne, noted for its lavender, at 8.30 a.m. yesterday morning [11 July] our destination on this 10th stage was Nice. We had 157 miles to do and, consequently, the pace was fairly steady. Occasionally, someone would try to make a breakaway but the *peloton* soon caught them. Nothing very exciting happened until after we had arrived at Nice for the first time. Here, we had fresh supplies of food and drink and were then sent on a detour of about 62 miles. My derailleur had been giving me a little trouble, the chain had jumped three or four times, and on each occasion I had to stop and then chase the field. The different sprockets, which are put on our machines almost every day according to the type of country to be negotiated, alter the control of the gear.

It was very hot, and as the promoters of this race had apparently picked out all the mountainous roads they could find for that detour from Nice, there were times when I felt like falling off and staying off, but the down-hill stretches are certainly a rest for one's legs, although a greater strain on the arms and nerves. But I felt better towards the end, and overtook a few riders who were taking 'acid' (amphetemines). Our old friend Goujon was one of these, and although he is very fast, the longer journeys and the mountains seem to take it out of him.

Cycling's report, 14 July

The speeds being registered stage by stage in the year's Tour are faster than ever before. This speeding up is more than one would expect as a result of the normal development in riding ability that is demonstrated year by year in the classic races and the record-breaking world. The faster times are explained by the experts as being solely due to the use of the variable gear for the first time this year. The mountains are being climbed at greater speed even by the tail end of the field …

The increased pace has resulted in a higher percentage of retirements. At Digne, only one stage before the halfway point of the race, 36 riders out of the original 98 had been eliminated, and amongst these were men whose names are famous throughout Europe for their road-riding ability. Charles Holland, a team of one – hill climber, stayer and sprinter combined – has had to keep pace with this, the fastest Tour de France ever, has had to overcome his troubles alone, and has had to plan his riding day by day, so that he reaches the Control before it closes. That he has done these tremendous tasks successfully thus so far, and that for the past six race days he has improved his position consistently in the general classification, provides evidence, if such be needed, of his courage and all-round riding skill.

THE HERO

Somewhere in France there rides a man and what a man is he
He's been there since the Tour began and at the end we hope he'll be.
His name is Charlie Holland and he rides for England's sake
So keep that in your mind Charlie, when your limbs begin to ache.
Remember when you're in the Alps, with the 'bonk' up to your eyes
You've got to capture many scalps, from those foreign guys.

They say you paced a motor-bike, but we know that's not true
You don't play those shady tricks, even if others do.
You're not the kind of bloke to whine being fined hundred francs
We suppose that great idea, came from some official crank
They put you at the back lad and made you bear the brunt
Perhaps they didn't like the thought of a newcomer at the front.

You may not be the first home, but even if you're the last
You've done something no other fellow has done in the past
They thought you were a mug lad, when you went out to try
But now you're leaving 'stars' behind you're making some of them cry
    So keep on trying Charlie, we're with you all the way
      Though it must be tough not understanding what other people say.

        We think of you each evening, towards the end of day
          'Let's hope he's still riding well', that is what we say.
            Just keep on going strong lad as you have done so far
            And you'll triumph just the same as when you won the BA
            And there'll be cyclists waiting to greet you by the score
            To greet our Charlie Holland, the hero of the Tour!

    Good luck Charlie
    The five well-wishers

Even in 1937, cyclists in the Tour de France were personalities. Charles received lots of fan mail from home and abroad wishing him *bon chance*. Five cyclists from Yorkshire wrote a poem for him, which must have put a smile on his face.

I have been very pleased to receive your nice photo.

I send you my best wishes for the new year. And I hope that you will be in the "Tour de France" of 1938.

I like all the sports: rowing, bycicle, ski. In this photo, I am rowing.

A French sportive girl
Nénette Malthier
Bacelle-Corrèze
(Corrèze)

Marseilles. July. 8th.

Bravo! Holland! We are some little frenchgirls, friends and admirers of the England, and I also, we are very glad to see an englishman in the bicycle-course.

What you are making (for a first time!) is a wonderful thing.

Next year you should come with a whole company and you should be the most powerful men.

Go on courageously and I shall go to cheer you at the "Arrival" in "Marseilles".

Bravo! Bravo, indeed! Boy!
Bravo! Boy!

with a friendly sympathy

Huguette

ANGOULÊME
18 — 12-VII
1937
CHARENTE

Mr. Charles Holland
Tour de France
Café de la Paix
rue Maguelar
(12.7.37)

Angoulême. 12.7.37

Dear Charlie,
Best of luck. Keep the old Union Jack flying. Am following your progress with great interest. A pity there aren't a few of the Yorkshire Road Club lads in the Tour. Keep on doing your best. Kindest regards, from a Yorkshireman in France.
John A. Whittle (Bradford)

VERVIERS (Belgique)
Centre d'Excursions
PAYS DE HERVE, HAUTES FAGNES,
ARDENNES.
Bureau de renseignements pour étrangers:
HÔTEL DE VILLE

Au moment du
Tour de France

Mr HOLLAND
aux bons soins du car-
cadis de Radio-Luxembourg.

Marseille
LUCRON
FRANCE

There were tremendous crowds at Nice, in fact all along the route. Puppo, the French rider, hails from Nice, and he was greeted with banners bearing the words 'Vive Puppo'. He made a big effort to win this stage, but was unable to overcome Vervaecke, and he finished 16th, three minutes behind the Belgian.

I was very glad when we had finished and could have a bath. No matter what the weather, we always arrive at the end of a stage covered with mud, dirt or tar. My position for this stage was 43rd in 8 hr. 42 min. 52 sec. Vervaecke's time being 8 hr. 29 min. 19 sec. In the general classification I was now 50th.

After the terrific climbs we have had during the past week we are enjoying another rest today. Nice is a beautiful place, but it is too hot to be comfortable. There are a few more stages we shall have to cover in the heat along the Riviera coast before we strike the Pyrenees. I have met one of two English boys touring, and

The Belgium team relaxing outdoors at their typically French hotel. Overnight accommodation was provided for teams, and Charles joined the Belgians.

other English people holidaying here. It is certainly encouraging to hear a good English yell now and again, although I get quite a lot of encouragement from the French people.

The stage from Nice to Marseilles on Tuesday last [13 July] was split into two sections. The first was a massed-start race of about 105 miles and, although we were off by eight o'clock in the morning, the sun was very bright and hot.

We started fairly leisurely, riding along the coast on a really good road. There were, as usual, thousands of specta-tors, and amongst them many beautiful bathing belles, sun-burned and sporting brief but brilliant swimsuits. Yes, at times it is very pleasant being a *coureur* [competitive cyclist] in the Tour de France!

We left the coast and found a few hills. The peacefulness was over. We were dancing, stamping, pulling, blowing and gasping. I found that my gears kept slipping and the chain came off and I was left behind. I started to chase the field but the clattering of the chain was getting on my

Whilst at Nice, Henri Desgrange, Editor of *L'Auto* and founder of the Tour, wrote about the riders. He said of Charles, 'Holland has all the characteristics of the English people, courage, tenacity, strength and a fine physique. I am happy to think that if the British wish to take part in road competitions on the Continent, they willl bring to the Tour de France a magnificent team, which will have the perseverance of the Belgians, the dash, the spirit and vigour of the Italians and the French. Let us never forget that, about fifty years ago, the British furnished us with the best road racers in the world.' Charles had covered the 1,382 miles to Nice in 70 hr. 39 min. 7 sec.. The leader of the Tour at this point was Sylvère Maes, whose time was 68 hr. 0 min. 37 sec.

At the feeding station, Charles collects his *musette* and refills his *bidons* (water bottles)

nerves. It came off again and I felt like throwing the machine over the hillside and packing up. I probably would have done if it had come off again, but after fiddling about with it I got the gear working much better, and then I came across Bartali also in trouble. Four Italians had stopped to get him back with the *peloton*, which was moving very fast, knowing that the Italians were in trouble. So I joined this small group and after a hard chase caught the field, only to discover that a few riders headed by Meulenberg had jumped away and they managed to keep ahead to the finish at Toulon.

We sat down to lunch in a large courtyard. We were given bread, vegetables, meat, fruit, mineral waters, beer, wine. This was some 'bun fight'. I had to pinch myself at times to make certain I was not dreaming. Dirty, sweaty, with eyes gleaming, jerseys torn, legs and arms bleeding, there they sat eating, their party manners forgotten, knowing that soon they would be again in the saddle, bashing away for all their worth.

The ride from Toulon to Marseilles was a time trial by teams. I found myself with the Italians, three Luxembourgers, and a Dutchman. I have mentioned already how the Italians sprint up the hills, and so I prepared for a hiding. It was very hard for the first hour, facing up the gradients, and every time the crowd shouted '*Vive l'Italien*' they made a special effort. One has to be ever on the alert to avoid disaster with this crowd. They switch about and one has to take the gutter or loose gravel in order to miss a smash. Once a rider touched a back wheel immediately in front of me and crashed; how I missed hitting him was a miracle.

I was riding quite strongly in the final hour. We had a little over 40 miles to go and several times, on hearing a yell, I turned round to find the Italians well in the rear, and I was actually waiting for them. Bartali did no pacemaking, and I shall be surprised if he stays in the race. [Bartali retired at the end of this stage suffering

Charles leads the *peloton* in the first half of the Marseilles-Montpellier stage in which he finished eleventh.

The chaotic scene at the level crossing between Nimes and Montpellier. Before Charles reached the gates the train came and he was held up.

with a fever as a result of his fall into the icy mountain torrent.]

I met quite a few English people at Marseilles, and it was a great pleasure to have a quiet chat with a fellow country-man.

On Wednesday the stage was again split into two races. The first was over 70 miles, from Marseilles to Nimes. The pace was very hot, like the sun, the riders constantly jumping and trying to break away from the field, and it was Antoine who managed to do so. I finished with the *peloton*. We had another alfresco lunch, this time in the bandstand of the local sports ground. The crowd got as near as the troops would allow, for we were guarded by battalions from the local barracks. Talk about watching the lions feed!

The second part of the stage was only 32 miles and it was a real sprint. So, as soon as the flag went down, the riders sprinted away. At about the halfway point there was a level crossing and half the field clambered over the bars which were down, but the other half were held up as the long train thundered by. I was with those held up and although afterwards we gave a hard chase, we could not catch the runaways before reaching Montpellier.

I suppose the idea of splitting the stages into two sections is to rest the riders over this hot part of the course. Whatever the reason, I cannot say I am in love with the idea. The riders go flat out most of the time on these short trips and one cannot get much shelter from the hot winds that sweep the roads unless a staggered party is formed.

The journey from Montpellier to Perpignan yesterday was similarly divided with 65 miles to do in the morning and 40 in the afternoon. The morning's race was a series of jumps interposed with long fast stretches. Through a winding village the Italian rider, Camusso, got away and stayed away for the *peloton* did not make a serious effort to overhaul him. The last five miles of the *demi-etape* was a hectic affair, everyone fighting for a position to contest the sprint, but the Belgians with their superior team work got Meulenberg over the line, first off the *peloton* and second to Camusso. I noticed in the newspaper report of this race that I am half way down the list of names finishing with the *peloton* and timed together, but I actually I finished in the sixth position, just behind Meulenberg.

Once more we had lunch in a bandstand, this time in the park at Narbonne. The enthusiasm of the crowd is now growing day by day. I ate and drank sparingly knowing that the pace would be terrible in the 40-mile run from Narbonne to Perpignan.

A group of eight riders jumped away immediately the flag was lowered. They included Choque, Meulenberg, and Bautz. I was with the peleton in hot pursuit, when my front tyre burst. I hurriedly changed, but was left behind. Chasing for an hour in the hot sun at the end of the day was a gruelling business, and I was very glad when I crossed the finishing line, although I was almost last. This has put me back a little in the general classification, my place being 51st.

Today we are resting at Perpignan, a very quaint old town with narrow and crooked streets. Our hotel, The Du Nord, was built apparently in an unorthodox style. It has a courtyard in the centre, high walls all round and balconies at each end. The unfortunate part about it is that people talk until a late hour in the courtyard, their voices echoing onto the open bedroom windows, and last night I found it impossible to sleep.

Each day I get lots of letters from Belgian and French people. It is amazing the knowledge everyone here has regarding the bicycle game. Even girls at school write to me, and their letters indicate a careful study of the Tour de France. One person in Belgium writes to say that their son has a Union Jack flying on the house and that it will be there as long as I am in the Tour. There are serious letters and amusing ones, but they all contain encouragement and wish me *bon chance*. I thank my English friends too, for the letters they have sent. I hope to reply to them all later. We must retire early tonight as the race starts at three o'clock in the morning!

A second letter from Walter, dated 14 July contained both advice and encouragement: 'I am pleased indeed to see that you are making such a good show in the Tour. At the same time and realising the difficulties you are up against, we should like to see you win a stage or two. According to the French papers, the Luchon to Pau stage in the Pyrenees is going to be the decisive one of the race and it will produce a battle royal between the Belgians and the Italians. You want to do your best to keep well up with them. However, do not take any risks as barring accidents you should now be able to finish, but if you can stage a get away in the half dozen concluding stages it would be much appreciated by us all.' The letter concluded with Walter explaining that he was taking his wife and daughter for a fortnight's holiday but was too busy to take a holiday himself. However, he still hoped to be at the finish and 'it would be great to see you first out of the bunch onto the Parc des Princes track. All the best and plenty of good luck.'

I retire but was abandoned first

Continuing my story: at 2 o'clock on the morning of 17 July we were awakened to prepare ourselves for the journey of 204 miles from Perpignan to Luchon. We had our usual breakfast of soup, fish, meat, ham, eggs, vegetables and fruit, with beer, wine, mineral waters and coffee to drink, and although we started at 4.00 a.m. and not 3.00 a.m. as stated in the programme, we left the town in darkness.

The procession wended its way through the town at about 15 mph, the riders joking and laughing with the spectators who, despite the early hour, were out in their thousands.

One or two spills occurred when the *peloton* tried to squeeze through bottleneck passages formed by farmer's carts and lorries pulled up on the roadside, taking their produce to town, but there was nothing serious.

At daybreak someone jumped away and the proceedings livened up considerably until the culprit was caught and told off for being so stupid trying to break away so early in the morning.

I had caught a slight cold and found my breathing not quite so good in the raw air of the early morning and when the big effort came halfway up the Mont-Louis I was content to stay with the back half of the *peloton* and finished the first part of the race three minutes behind Meulenberg, the winner. This was at Bourg-Madame, and after a brief rest we set off again, the second *étape* being to Ax-les-Thermes. I climbed the Col de Puymorens much better and was in a good position halfway down when I felt my back wheel bumping. The roads had been quite good up to there, and as I had heavy tyres on I was rather surprised to puncture; but I found I had picked up a large stud.

After changing tyres I set off after the Belgian, Wierinckx, who was about a minute in front and, after a hard chase, caught him.

Wierinckx worked with me in trying to reduce our arrears, and although I consider I went faster over this 20 mile stretch than I had done on any similar distance during the Tour, we finished a little over three minutes behind Canardo, who was successful in the sprint at Ax-les-Thermes.

Whilst I sat down to lunch in a cafe's pleasant garden, a mechanic put a new sticky tape on the back rim, as I had felt the tyre that I had changed creep a little on the hairpin bends.

It is very unpleasant when a tyre comes off doing the knots down the mountains, and by attending to these details much trouble and many accidents are avoided.

As in the previous stages that day, the third and final one to Luchon started very sedately, and I kept at the front thinking that for once I would really force myself when we came to the mountains. When we were in the Alps I used to ease off when it became hard, as I did not know my capabilities as a climber, and being in the first section of the field with many well known riders behind I became frightened lest I should crack and be unable to finish the Tour; but having done the Alps without unduly distressing myself I felt justified in my present plan of action.

The first mountain on this stage is the Col de Port, so when Vervaecke, Berrendero, Vicini, Maes and the other climbing specialists started to make their attacks I kept close by them and was only 30 yards behind the leader a short way from the top when I punctured again. I should still have been with the tail of the field if my pump had worked properly. It had been okay in the morning but I think the heat had probably affected the washer; whatever it was I could only get the tyre half-hard, and after bumping along for a short distance I managed to get another pump from an English speaking pressman, and put more wind in the tyre. I was soon over the top of the col, but coming down the other side

I had two more punctures, and as we only carry two spares I could do nothing but wait for something to turn up.

A crowd of peasants had gathered round me, but they could not help me. A priest brought me a bottle of beer, and although it quenched my thirst it got me no further. Outwardly I probably appeared calm, but I was furious, I could not imagine another 'Ace' being left like this. In fact some riders have spare wheels complete with tyres given them by officials when they puncture.

Charles takes a drink on the stage before his enforced retirement.

It seemed ages after I had given up hope that a tourist came along and gave me a tubular touring tyre. I put it on, and in the excitement the rod of the second pump broke. We blew it hard with another pump, but the tyre fitted so loosely on the rim that it came off with the fingers and was unsafe to ride. Another tyre was found, which fitted a little better, and again I set off towards Luchon, but I had by then given up hope, and when I arrived at Saint-Girons, where the Control was, and where we were to receive a 'musette' of food and drink, the officials had gone, and I took my number off and retired. I had lost anything from three-quarters of an hour to an hour, and knowing the fate of Bill Burl and other riders who were so placed, I felt it was a waste of effort to carry on racing.

I had of course, to get to Luchon, so when I saw a press car with the official badge I asked them for a lift, but they said 'No' and offered me some spare tyres. I told them I did not want the tyres and that I had retired and only wanted to get to Luchon. They would not give me a lift but drove alongside trying their hardest to persuade me to carry on, and even grabbed me by the jersey and pulled me along from the car, saying that it would be all right in view of the extraordinary circumstances.

I was definitely retired, and after being penalised at the beginning of the Tour, I have been most careful not to infringe any regulations since, so I put on the brakes and stopped and there they left me. They said afterwards that they thought I would carry on, if they left me alone. I think they would have done anything to have kept me in the Tour; but I did not wish to finish this great race unless it was by my own efforts I finally received a lift by a private car, and thus ended the Tour de France for me!

There have been many stories in the various papers about my retirement, the French journalists in particular writing their articles with a great deal of imagination. Firstly, stories regarding my manager – I had no manager. Then how I went to see Monsieur Desgrange to see if I could ride the next stage and complete the Tour – I wouldn't dream of such a thing.

I had to smile when I saw the headlines in another paper, 'How peasants tried to keep lone Briton in World's Greatest Race'. I was supposed to have been pushed from village to village for miles!

I have been asked if I will come back next year; my answer was, 'if I come back next year it must be with a full team and an English and French speaking manager'.

Cycling magazine reported:

Opinion is unanimous that Charles Holland's performance in the Tour de France does him infinite credit. To ride nearly 2,000 miles in such company, over strange and immensely difficult roads, in a

From the outset, Charles was regarded as good 'copy'. Cartoonists seized on the opportunity of depicting something unique, an Englishman in the Tour. This one shows him wearing a top hat and carrying a toothbrush.

la Gazett

LE TOUR VU A TRAVERS LES LUNETTES ROSES

Bye, bye, Holland !

par **Robert PERRIE**

BAGNERES-DE-LUCHON, 17 juil — Charles Holland n'est pas arrivé, soir, sur les allées d'Etigny. Nous ne verrons plus, sur la route, sa fine silhouette de jeune lord échappé d'un ford pour courir à bicyclette. Nous reverrons plus son sourire discret, coups d'œil malicieux. Nous n'entendrons plus ses réflexions puisées aux sources du meilleur humour de son pays. Nous allons lui rendre, demain, le pyjama qu'il nous avait lancé dans notre voiture, après Lille, avec sa brosse à dents et sa pâte dentifrice... et qu'il ne nous avait jamais plus réclamés. Charles Holland a abandonné le Tour de France tout à l'heure, avant le col du Portet d'Aspet. Il a abandonné sans taper avec une morgue hautaine, c'est juste s'il n'a pas tiré de sa musette la pipe de « Navy Cut » pour la fumer paisiblement sur le bord de la route, en mettant sur les caprices du sort. Sans doute que Charles Holland n'aime pas se le tôt. Toujours est-il que, pour une fois qu'il a transgressé ses principes pour raisons majeures, il a connu toutes les misères qui peuvent compliquer la vie d'un honnête coureur cycliste. Cela commença par le petit ennui du dérailleur, qui lui perdre un temps précieux, puis son pneu creva. Holland est un sage. Il répare renfourcha son vélo déréglé et reprit son petit bonhomme de chemin en continuant les paysages de la Tamise à ceux de l'Ariège. Mais il creva une seconde fois. Il creva une troisième fois ! C'était l'abomination de la désolation, d'autant plus que — comble des combles — sa pompe était cassée, à son tour. Charles Holland en bon Britannique, eut une première réaction — la première.

« Comment, moi, sujet de plus grand roi du monde, je vais être la risée tout le monde en passant une demi-heure après mes camarades ! Sûr mon maillot je porte l'étendard de l'Union Jack. Je n'ai pas le droit de déshonorer mon pays. Je dois abandonner. »

La nouvelle fusa dans la caravane. On donna à notre ami Raymond Thumazeul, du « Jour », deux boyaux pour l'infortuné Holland, mais celui-ci les refusa systématiquement, parce que Thoum n'est pas officiel et qu'il craignait de contre venir au règlement.

Un peu plus tard, M. Bélias, le mécène de La Vie, arriva à la rescousse avec Georges Vikar, le benjamin de Radio-Luxembourg, qui s'est intitulé directeur technique de l'équipe de Grande-Bretagne (on ne peut rien montrer aux enfants). le bébé Vikar, qui, sur le marchepied de la voiture de La Vie, faisant une invitation parfaite de Jean Leuillot venant parler aux oreilles de Lapébie, vint exhorter Holland, le suppliant de continuer, et allant jusqu'à lui dire : « Je t'en supplie, fais ça pour moi ! » Cette jeunesse ne doute de rien. Mais, à Saint-Girons, le boyau plat, le front soucieux, Charley héla une voiture qui passait et rentra à Luchon par le plus court chemin.

Tout à l'heure, il a tenté une ultime démarche auprès du Père du Tour. Mais le règlement est le règlement : un coureur qui ne se fait pas chronométrer à l'arrivée d'une étape ne peut pas repartir le lendemain. Ça serait vraiment trop facile. Nous avons donc perdu le sympathique petit Anglais de notre caravane, et c'est lui qui, ce soir, porte le deuil de son Tour de France, ce Tour de France qu'il aimait tant et qu'il compte bien refaire l'année prochaine. C'est là grâce que je lui souhaite.

A bientôt, « old chap, bye, bye, Holland ! ».

foreign country where he could not depend upon making himself understood, is a feat that is not adequately recognised by merely writing it down as a failure. Holland did not win, did not even finish, but he outlasted many riders with far more experience than himself, and showed conclusively that if he were teamed with some of the best talent at this highly specialised game, instead of being left to plough a more or less lonely furrow, he would be capable of carrying off the highest honours of the Tour.

At Luchon, where Charles had retired, Maes of Belgium, was the leader with Lapébie of France, second. The next stage from here to Pau, which Walter had written to Charles about, was actually won by a Spaniard, Berrendo, with Maes and Lapébie finishing in a group 49 seconds behind him. Lapébie was given second place but he was penalised 90 seconds for being assisted uphill by spectators. In the Yellow Jersey stakes he was still second but he threatened to abandon taking the rest of the French team with him. The following day, the last rest day before Paris, they changed their minds!

Maes retained a 25-second lead over Lapébie in the 16th stage from Pau to Bordeaux but bad feeling between the two teams was coming to a head. The next morning saw an unprecedented event when Maes and the rest of the Belgian team withdrew from the Tour. The Belgians alleged that a stone was thrown at them bringing down one of their riders. They also said pepper was thrown in the eyes of another and that a level crossing gate was deliberately closed to prevent Maes, who was delayed by a puncture, from catching Lapébie.

Only 46 riders set off on the next stage but four days later over half-a-million people welcomed them back to Paris. Roger Lapébie of France came first, beating the Italian, Mario Vincini, by 7 minutes, with Léo Amberg of Switzerland coming third, ahead of Francesco Camusso of Italy.

The Tour was described in the editorial of *Cycling* as a sorry affair and that:

So far as this country is concerned the race this year has had one outstanding justification; it has shown us the courage and the splendid riding ability of one of our own men, Charles Holland. We can take pride in his glorious failure knowing that alone as he was, a complete stranger in his

Lapébie leading the field into Bordeaux. Maes who was behind, having punctured, was, it is alleged, still further hindered by spectators.

surroundings, the victor's laurels could never have been his had he been the greatest stayer, the fastest sprinter and the finest roadmen in the race. Holland is the product of his own determination to be the best Englishman at that class of riding. That he kept in the Tour for three-quarters of the distance, and was only them forced to abandon through ill-luck demonstrates that no matter what the sphere of competitive cycling we have ambitions to contest, men can be developed, if we have the will, who can again rank with the world's best.

The Bicycle said: 'Goodbye Holland. Do not be discouraged by your bad luck. You are the man of the Tour.'

Robert Perrier wrote in *L'Auto*:

Charles Holland did not arrive on the avenues of Etigny. We will no longer see his fine youthful silhouette on the road. We will no longer see his modest smile and his mischievous glances. We will no longer hear his humorous reflections. Tomorrow we will give him the pyjamas he threw in our car after Lille along with his toothbrush and toothpaste, which he never reclaimed. Charles Holland has abandoned the Tour without a fuss and with pride.'

All Charles said was that he was fitter when he was forced to retire than when he started.

It was not until 1955, 18 years after Charles' ride, that a team of British riders competed in the Tour. Dave Bedwell, Stan Jones, Fred Krebs, Bob Maitland, Ken Mitchell, Bernard Pusey, Brian Robinson, Tony Hoar, Ian Steel and Bevis Wood formed the Hercules team. Brian Robinson and Tony Hoar both finished. One can only imagine what Charles could have done with such a group supporting him.

Charles, resting in the car after finishing his Land's End–London record-breaking ride. This was his third attempt, and he convincingly beat Opperman's time by twenty-five minutes.

CHAPTER 8
Ticket to ride

The first few months of the year was always a quiet time for the cycling magazines published at this time and 1938 was no exception. *Cycling* decided to overcome the lack of racing reports with a feature entitled, The Physical Attributes of the Famous and Others. by Charles Fearnley, Famous Health Expert.

Of Charles he wrote:

Charles Holland. Aristocrat among British cyclists. BAR, Tour de France an' all that. Swarthy and sleek, a lovely physique – no, I hardly intended that to rhyme, although it is more than appropriate, for this body before us is rhythm and poetry to the body culturist. Symmetrical as Mother Nature in her kindliest mood can fashion, Charles Holland's rich dark skin covers curves and ripples of mighty, but not massive muscularity, which only the eye and not the rule can measure and appreciate.

Surprisingly, there was no speculation in the magazines as to a team or even riders for the 1938 Tour de France. The previous July, whilst Charles was still riding in the Tour, he received several letters from W. Morgan Williams who lived near Paris and was amongst other things a sporting journalist. The first letter said: 'When you get back to Paris we can have a talk about next year's race. It may be possible that I can raise the cash for this.' In his next letter he referred to what Desgrange had written about Charles (see page 141) and wrote:

This makes it hopeful for next year, thanks to your fine performance, and we should get together immediately so as to form that very team he needs. You cannot say that it is anything less than an invitation to dance. I mean race. What is your private opinion of the matter? Don't you think we could pull it off together?

A further letter sent to Charles from Morgan Williams stated:

I am already on the job for next year and next month will sent along prices for putting up ten lads in a camp for training purposes. It is a very serious outfit but I have arranged that the boys should have Mondays off to do as they please. There are plenty of switch back roads around and the air is the best, also it is not far from Paris.

Interestingly, Morgan Williams also commented on the threatened withdrawal of the French team from the Tour in 1937 when Lapébie was fined, 'Ol' man Desgrange would have had them disqualified for insubordination for twelve to eighteen months.' A good enough reason for second thoughts!

The final letter written by him on 29 December 1937 said: 'I am doing my best to get the money to have a full team in the 1938 Tour. It is very difficult but I hope to win out.' Whether his best was not good enough, or whether Charles' professional commitments meant a team could not be formed, is unknown but we do know that it was not until 1955, 18 years after Charles' ride, that a team of British riders competed in the Tour.

Charles had to wait patiently until June 1938 for the chance of a Road Records Association attempt. He was particularly keen to attack the Lands End to London record as he thought that the hill-climbing experience gained in the Tour de France would stand him in good stead. It did, but not over this course; it was the Liverpool to Edinburgh which provided him with his first professional record. Charles knocked 12 minutes off the previous record, held for three years by Frank Southall, mainly due to his ability to 'make dashing hill climbs, dancing on the pedals and hardly ever slowing to a crawl even on the steepest gradient'. The Lake District must have seemed relatively easy after the Alps. He covered the 210 miles from the Post Office in Liverpool to the Post Office in Edinburgh in 9 hrs. 59 min. 11 sec., which was rounded up to 10 hours. As the advert for Raleigh and Sturmey-Archer 3-speed gears says, 'Just think what this means!'.

In August he had the opportunity of attacking the Australian Hubert Opperman's 1935 record for the 287 miles from Lands End to London, and what a ride it was. He left Lands End at 8.15 a.m. and in less than half an hour at Penzance was soaked by heavy rain. The first 50 miles were covered in 2 hr. 13 min. but then he began to slow down. It was a holiday weekend and on the narrow roads, processions of cars crawled, at little more than a cyclist's pace in both directions, creating a nightmare of fumes and dust. Subsequently, Charles suffered from sickness. The traffic congestion took its toll and at Wincanton he was 21 minutes behind the set schedule. Charles pressed on and by Basingstoke the sickness had passed, the traffic had calmed down, and he was pedalling like his old self. However, on the outskirts of London, when he stopped for a break, he was still behind schedule and it looked like the end of the attempt. Wrapped in a rug Charles asked how far was left, '29 miles', was the reply, 'how much time left?' – '67 min.', he was told. 'Well, give me a drink. I can still do it' and

with that he flung off the rug, snatched his bike, took a gulp of his drink and pedalled off into the night heading through Staines, Hounslow and into London like a bat out of hell. He related it thus: 'I rode like one possessed. I dodged in and out of traffic. Taxi drivers swore at me as I swung by, just missing pedestrians. I was soon through Hammersmith and Kensington, and I didn't stop for anything until I made my final sprint to Hyde Park gates. I had done what I said I would do.' Described as one of the most skilful and inspiring 23 miles' ride imaginable, Charles arrived at Hyde Park Corner to find quite a crowd waiting to welcome him. Tension mounted waiting for the timekeeper's announcement. Charles had completed this dramatic ride of 287 miles in 14 hr. 8 min. 19 sec. Unfortunely, he had failed by 19 seconds to beat Opperman's record (14 hr. 9 min.), as a full minute was the smallest unit of time recognised in records.

Before Charles had the chance to attempt this record again it was the World's Championship in Amsterdam and Valkenburg at the end of August and the beginning of September. Charles rode in the professional road race but, unfortunately, crashed in the third lap. After several delays caused by trying to get his rear wheel properly adjusted, he rode on for a further five laps, but retired when he was seven minutes behind. He had also injured his knee and this prevented him riding in the Grand Prix des Nations. This was a great shame as it was the first time a British rider had been invited to ride in this famous race.

However, his luck was changing, ironically, with the number 13. It was on 13 October when Charles eventually smashed Opperman's Lands End to London record, covering the 287 miles in 13 hr. 44 min., beating the record not by 1 minute but by 25 minutes! This was his third attempt as a second one had been called off due to inclement weather. The story is told here in his own words.

    "The night before the record attempt 13 of us were about to sit down to a meal. One of the helpers said he'd have his later, but I insisted that 13 was my lucky number, and so it proved. Conditions were favourable when I started at the door of the Lands End Hotel. Except for the sea mist, which reduced visibility in places, a good breeze helped me along and the first check at Penzance showed I was inside my schedule.

A shower of rain came and I needed a little more care at the bends. The straight stretches over Bodmin Moor gave me a further chance to improve on schedule, and the hard tyres were humming merrily until a sharp flint deflated my back tyre just outside Launceston. A spare was quickly unstrapped from the following car and I didn't lose much time. The hub ratio of 71-81-92 were just right for the undulating roads in Cornwall and Devon, between Okehampton and Exeter, with

Charles takes yet another drink, this time during the Land's End–London record ride in 1938. In the 1930s, it seems that when cyclists slow down for a drink, photographers take the opportunity of snapping them!

the sun shining and dry roads. Devon became truly glorious and I was frequently having rides of 40 mph.

The road changes course at Ilminster where the rain fell again, and the wind, which had been helpful, now appeared to be against me. Battle really commenced. A hold up on a stretch of one-way traffic for road repairs was very frustrating, but at Mere, with the conditions improving, I was still on level terms with the schedule.

The sun, which again appeared, but getting lower in the sky, encouraged my efforts, for I knew I had little more than an hour of daylight, and the run along the fringes of the Salisbury plain was probably the best effort of my whole ride.

I was flat out mile after mile, and the drinks, which were handed up with perfect regularity, at the agreed spot were never more appreciated. I was rarely doing below 25 mph and frequently around 35 mph.

Lighting up time came with about 80 miles to go, and again the rain with it, making it impossible to maintain my previous progress.

The worst stretch was between Andover and Basingstoke where I found the hilly, twisting road nerve racking, especially on a descent, being able to see only a few yards in front.

I was not unduly worried by this, as I knew the schedule had allowed for slowing down over the last 50 miles, and with straight flat roads ahead I felt quite cheerful. Passing the spot at Camberly where I had almost exploded two months before, I knew barring accidents it was 'in the bag'. I wasn't quite as fast over the last few miles as on the other ride, but I was still riding faster than the schedule had allowed for, and with groups of club folk now appearing and encouraging me on, the miles seemed to fly by.

With only two more miles to do and feeling on top of the world I punctured! The official car had passed by some time before to get the timekeeper to the finish, and the second car had been unable to keep up with me in the London traffic. To my considerable relief some kind

Approaching Hyde Park corner on the successful Land's End–London ride, on a borrowed bike after puncturing.

soul offered me a bike and although it was about six inches too big for me, and equipped with everything a tourist could want it did the job of getting me to Hyde Park Corner.

What a thrill! A ride so full of incidents, too many to enumerate here, and some that could have spelled disaster. But with confidence and determination from the start, and perfect organisation from my Raleigh sponsors and Lady Luck, I had beaten the bogey which had seemed to dominate my earlier efforts. I don't think I have ever enjoyed a glass of beer more than the one sitting in the car at Hyde Park Corner, but what a relief to reach the hotel and get rid of those tights, which had been soaked and then dried on me many times that day.

Incidentally, I noticed the number on the door as I walked into that hotel. Guess what it was. Yes, number 13.

Towards the end of March 1939 the Raleigh-Sturmey-Archer team, Sid Ferris, Bert James and of course Charles, moved into Donington Hall, in North West Leicestershire adjacent to the well known motor racing and massed-start racing circuit. The plan was that they trained together using the track for speed work and the country lanes for the longer distance training rides. They were aiming not only to retain the records they held but to increase that number. Between them they already held nine of the fifteen recognised road records.

By June, Charles was superbly fit and waiting to attack the Edinburgh to York record, held for four years by Frank Southall. Many riders, including Charles in 1936, had tried and failed in their effort to crack this record and favourable weather was considered a must to do so. The schedule for Charles' attempt included two other records, that of Edinburgh to London and the 24-hour.

The day arrived when it was thought the weather would be kind and the wind from the right direction. Charles' exceptional climbing ability again stood him in good stead. On leaving Edinburgh the course was uphill for over 18 miles. In true Tour de France style, he tackled these hills keeping up an average speed of 21 mph.

He crossed the border in to England looking as fit as at the start and ahead of his time schedule. It was here the wind changed and instead of a wind from the north west an east wind blew. As the road went in a south-easterly direction, this was almost as bad as a head wind. By Newcastle, where Charles had to jump off his bike and run with it a few yards to get around a traffic jam caused by a brewers dray, Charles was four minutes behind his schedule.

A steam tractor with a wire cable pulling a tree trunk across the road necessitated the next quick dismount. Whether Charles would beat the record was now touch and go. He approached York very close to it, but still had to negotiate two sets of traffic lights and the narrow twisting streets crowded with traffic. Any second lost could make all the difference. It was said that under such conditions Charles was at his best and that he weaved his way through the streets in a way that would have made any London cab driver green with envy.

Charles had instructions not to stop at York so he sped through the time control unaware of whether he had broken the record. It was 22 miles south of York when Charles was called to a halt. His time for the 186¾ miles was 8 hr. 36 min. This time Lady Luck was on his side, he had beaten the record by one minute. With the sun beating down mercilessly, and the east wind freshening all the time, the chances of the other two records seemed vague. A disappointed Charles did not continue. As the report in *The Bicycle* said: 'The dusky Midlander, now sunburnt to a mahogany shade, rested content with the Edinburgh to York record but confident that with better weather conditions he can get the two longer distance records [the Edinburgh–London and the 24-hour].'

With the outbreak of the Second World War this was not to be, and this was Charles' last record for the next thirty years.

Afterword
WITH ALL DUE RESPECT

Charles married Mary Phyllis Flack of Walsall on 10 November 1940 and in 1943 was called for military service in the Royal Signal Corps. His occupation on entry was recorded as a professional cyclist and, staying on the road, he became a driver and mechanic. His trips through France and Germany were in circumstances so totally different to his previous visits in the 1930s; it must have been extremely difficult for him. On his discharge in October 1946, he concentrated on building up his newsagent and grocery business.

Cycling links were maintained for a short while, when Charles acted as racing secretary for the MC&AC. He was no longer able to compete in amateur cycle racing, because at the time cycling's governing body ruled that once you had been a professional you could not revert to amateur status. This rule applied to anyone who had been a professional in whatever sport. (Charles knew an ex-professional boxer who wished to take up cycle racing as a vet but was not allowed to do so.) Therefore, the bike was only used as a means of transport until it was replaced by a car. Phyl (his wife) was a keen tennis player and for many years tennis was the only sport Charles played.

As his three daughters (Pauline, Frances and Nina) grew up and with more time to spare, another game was added to his repertoire – golf. The same determination and dedication was given to this as he would to any other sport and in a short time he was playing off a single-figure handicap in pro-am tournaments. As Charles said, 'Golf is a great game and it has the same appeal as cycling. You don't need a lot of people with you and like cycling you can practise quietly on your own for hours.'

In December 1962 Charles was invited as a guest, along with Phyl and his daughters, to speak in what was now called The Champions' Concert and Prize Presentation in the Albert Hall. The format remained similar to that of thirty years previous, with Tommy Trinder as the compere, and the same mix of jugglers, dancers, singers, clowns and acrobats. Charles' speech formed part of 'The Story of a Yellow Jersey'. Tom Simpson, Louison and Jean Bobet,

Bad weather didn't prevent Charles from training; he would simply put a set of rollers in the dining room. Here he is using his preferred Major Nichols bike.

Brian Robinson and Jaques Godet, the successor of Henri Desgrange also took part in this event, with Simpson presenting the prizes. Frank Colden was the men's BAR, with an average speed for the three distances of 24.652 mph, and Beryl Burton (for '25', '50' and a '100') was the women's BAR in 24.036 mph. Charles' time in 1936 was 22.097 mph.

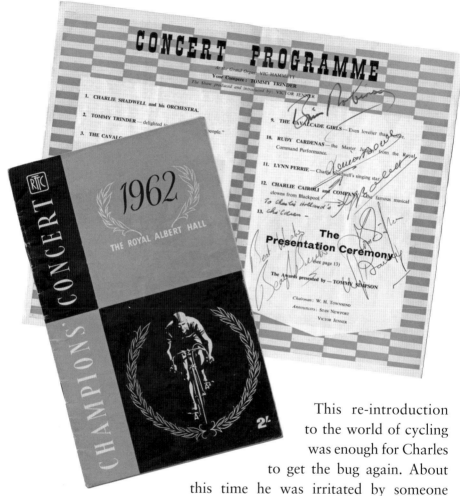

This re-introduction to the world of cycling was enough for Charles to get the bug again. About this time he was irritated by someone saying that he wouldn't ever be able to get back into racing form. Charles replied, 'With all due respect, I can and I will, if I decide to.' He sorted a bike out and went for a ride only to realise how unfit he was. Sadly, Walter had died suddenly in 1960 of a heart attack. His untimely death had really shocked Charles and must also have influenced his decision to get fit.

Over the next few years he lost weight and stopped smoking, and very soon cycling became more important than golf. In 1963 he accepted an invitation to become president of the MC&AC, a post he held for three years. He joined the Veterans Time Trial Association in 1966 but had to wait until 1968 before he could race again. This was when the ruling allowing ex-professionals to compete as amateurs was changed.

'Holland Storms Back in Style', read the headline of an article about one of Charles' first races in 1968. This was a 100-mile time trial in Berkshire, which he won in 4 hr. 45 min. at the age of 59.

By the 1970s Charles was training daily and, as in the past, keeping records of the distance covered, where he had been, and the time it had taken. Averaging 200 miles a week, Charles set up 'rollers' in his dining room so that inclement weather would not affect his schedule.

It was in 1974, at the age of 65, Charles first entered and won the VTTA BAR with the previous year's winner, Harry Hill, coming second. Charles relished this win over his main rival and about Harry he said: 'We're the best of pals. We met about five or six years ago for the first time since we rode in the 1936 Olympics when Harry was third in the team pursuit. Harry's got some wonderful ideas, next year he wants us both to go abroad and challenge veterans around the world!'

Charles didn't make it abroad in 1975, although he did make it to the Isle of Man, his first visit there since 1936 when he won the inaugural Manx International Bicycle Race. 'Charlie turns the clock back', 'Holland is back 39 years later', 'Charlie is still a winner at 66' – these quotes from the press say it all. He won the VTTA 25-mile time trial in 1hr. 7 min 2 sec.. This race was part of what had become an International Cycling Week, held the week after the Isle of Man TT motorcycle racing event, with hundreds of cyclists visiting the island. Eighty veterans had taken part in the time trial.

Charles became champion veteran time triallist in 1975 for the second time, achieving age-related records for the four distances. His times were 1 hr. 2 min. 23 sec. for the '25', 2 hr. 10 min. 46 sec. for the '50', and 4 hr. 23 min. 46 sec. for the '100'. In the 12-hour he completed 242.11 miles. This was less than the previous year when he was a mile short of his personal best. Charles felt he could do better in a '25' if he picked the right course on the

In 1972 at 63 years, Charles' VTTA Age Records were: 25 miles, 1 hr. 1 min. 23 sec., 50 miles, 2 hr. 9 min. 6 sec., and 100 miles, 4 hr. 40 min. 47 sec.

right day. In a private trial he did 59 minutes, a personal best at 66 years old, and he was keen to achieve under the hour in an open event. When asked about his improved times he laughed and said he thought it unbelievable. He put it down to better conditions, the bikes and better 'know-how' in training. He also thought: 'When you're younger you tend to indulge yourself in the social season. Especially myself – I had a lot of social functions to attend being in the cycle trade.'

Charles continued cycling for several years, often meeting up with his brothers, Alf and Jack, for runs from Aldridge, around the surrounding countryside, and to old haunts such as Lichfield or Tamworth. Tuesday was a regular 'night out with the lads' when cycling past and present was the main topic of conversation.

On 26 January 1988 Charles attended an unique gathering of Olympians held at Buckingham Palace and hosted by HRH The Princess Royal (Princess Anne), an Olympian herself. The event was held to promote and raise the profile of the British Olympic Association and British sport at home and internationally. Princess Anne presented more than 200 commemorative pins to the guests, as a further reminder of their sporting achievements, and chatted amiably to them all. As she said the historic event was also 'an excuse for a jolly good party'.

Phyl died in 1988 and Charles died in 1989, aged 81. Over fifty years previously, in 1936, at a dinner held in his honour by four Midland cycling clubs, jokes were made as to what plot of earth would claim Charles for its own, Birmingham, Walsall, or Aldridge. The latter won; he is buried in the family grave at St Mary's Parish Church, Aldridge. Survived by his three daughters and eight grand-children, he leaves behind his memories and achievements recorded here.

British cyclists in the Tour de France

The following list shows the 57 British riders who have competed in the Tour (up until 2007); 26 of these riders finished the race and they have their positions after their name. Several riders have finished more than once.

1937 Bill Burl, Charles Holland

   During the years 1938–1954 no British riders entered

1955 Dave Bedwell, Tony Hoar (69th), Stan Jones, Fred Krebs, Bob Maitland, Ken Mitchell, Bernard Pusey, Brian Robinson (29th), Bevis Wood, Ian Steel
1956 Brian Robinson (14th)
1957 Brian Robinson
1958 Stan Brittain (69th), Ron Coe, Brian Robinson
1959 John Andrews, Tony Hewson, Brian Robinson (19th), Victor Sutton (37th)
1960 John Andrews, Stan Brittain, John Kennedy, Harry Reynolds, Brian Robinson (26th), Norman Sheil, Tom Simpson (29th), Victor Sutton
1961 Stan Brittain, Ron Coe, Vin Denson, Albert Hitchen, Kenneth Laidlaw (65th), Ian Moore, George O'Brien, Brian Robinson (53rd), Peter Ryall, Sean Ryan, Tom Simpson
1962 Alan Ramsbottom (45th), Tom Simpson (6th)
1963 Alan Ramsbottom (16th)
1964 Vin Denson (72nd), Barry Hoban (65th), Tom Simpson (14th), Michael Wright (56th)
1965 Vin Denson (87th), Tom Simpson, Michael Wright (24th)
1966 Vin Denson, Tom Simpson
1967 Peter Chisman, Vin Denson, Peter Hill, Albert Hitchen, Barry Hoban (62nd), Bill Lawrie, Colin Lewis (84th), Arthur Metcalfe (69th), Tom Simpson, Michael Wright

1968	Robert Addy, John Clarey (63rd), Vin Denson (62nd), Derek Green, Derek Harrison, Barry Hoban (33rd), Colin Lewis, Arthur Metcalfe, Hugh Porter, Michael Wright (28th)
1969	Derek Harrison (32nd), Barry Hoban (67th), Michael Wright (71st)
1970	Barry Hoban
1971	Barry Hoban (41st)
1972	Barry Hoban (70th), Michael Wright (55th)
1973	Barry Hoban (43rd), Michael Wright (57th)
1974	Barry Hoban (37th), Michael Wright (57th)
1975	Barry Hoban (68th)
1976	No British riders
1977	Bill Nickson, Barry Hoban (41st)
1978	Barry Hoban (65th), Paul Sherwen (70th)
1979	Paul Sherwen (81st)
1980	Graham Jones (49th), Paul Sherwen
1981	Graham Jones (20th), Paul Sherwen
1982	Paul Sherwen (111th)
1983	Graham Jones (69th), Robert Millar (14th)
1984	Graham Jones, Robert Millar (4th), Paul Sherwen (116th), Sean Yates (91st)
1985	Robert Millar (11th), Paul Sherwen (141st) Sean Yates (122nd)
1986	Robert Millar, Sean Yates (112th)
1987	Malcolm Elliot (94th) Graham Jones, Robert Millar (19th), Adrian Timmis (70th), Paul Watson, Sean Yates
1988	Malcolm Elliot (90th), Sean Yates (59th), Robert Millar
1989	Robert Millar, Sean Yates (45th)
1990	Robert Millar, Max Sciandri (154th), Sean Yates (119th)
1991	Robert Millar (72nd), Sean Yates
1992	Robert Millar (18th), Max Sciandri, Sean Yates (83rd)
1993	Robert Millar (24th), Max Sciandri (71st), Sean Yates (88th)
1994	Chris Boardman, Sean Yates (71st)
1995	Chris Boardman, Max Sciandri (47th), Sean Yates
1996	Chris Boardman (39th)
1997	Chris Boardman, Max Sciandri (67th)
1998	Chris Boardman, Max Sciandri
1999	Chris Boardman (119th)
2000	David Millar (62nd)
2001	David Millar
2002	David Millar (68th)
2003	David Millar (55th)
2004	No British riders
2005	No British riders
2006	David Millar
2007	Mark Cavendish, David Millar (69th), Geraint Thomas (140th), Charly Wiegelius (45th) and Bradley Wiggins

Index

Acknowledgements

My sincere thanks go to: my sister Nina, without whom the book would never have made it;
Martin for his patience and lovely book design, and all at M&N publishing;
Fiona McKenna for typing the original memoirs;
Melissa Spencer and Claire Sherwin – the proof readers;
Hugh Porter for the Foreword and cheering us up;
and last, but not least, my family and friends who have helped in many ways, and have put up with me 'going on' about the book.

Bye, bye, Holland!

Sorry Dad any modesty you may have had has now gone out of the window!

Picture credits

The author and publisher would like to thank Cycling Weekly for supplying photographs and for their permission to reproduce copyright material. Every effort has been made to trace and credit all copyright holders, but we apologise should there have been any ommissions. Thanks also to The National Cycling Archive for their help with photographs.